THE SUPERNATURAL REALM

THE SUPERNATURAL REALM

Second Edition

Discover Heaven's Secrets

BILL VINCENT

Revival Waves of Glory, PO Box 596 Litchfield, IL 62056

http://www.revivalwavesofgloryministries.com/

Published in the United States of America

ISBN: 978-0692658154
1. Religion / Christian Life / Spiritual Growth
2. Religion / Christian Life / Personal Growth
14.07.28

TABLE OF CONTENTS

BOOK DISCLAIMER

Here are tips on reading Bill Vincent's Books.

Bill writes prophetically as God speaks. The grammar may be pushed but the message is spoken from the heart of God. Bill didn't want to lose the depth of revelation through extensive editing.

INTRODUCTION

It is amazing to me that I am even writing a book like this. It was just a few years ago that it was unclear to me what the supernatural is. I went through a season of the presence of God overtaken my life and brought supernatural favor, power, revelations, open visions and encounters with Heaven. Many are satisfied with a little touch of heaven. There are hidden things waiting to be discovered for such a time as this. Why wait until we die to have heavenly experiences.

I believe as you read this book the Heavens will open over your life, if you press in for more of the supernatural realm.

HEAVEN INVADING EARTH

There is at all times a sound being released from earth to heaven as well as from heaven to earth a divine exchange, so to speak. In the unseen realm, it is in the form of energy patterns, waves, particles and though the vast majority of it is not heard with our natural ear, it is sensed by us because we are part of this existence. What is coming from our end is "heard" by God, and I believe that He has an ever flowing response back to us that we need to be aware of and "tune into" with our spirit man so as to tap into that constant communion we can have with Him. We often refer to it, as does Scripture, as "spirit to spirit, deep to deep". In John 17, Jesus prays concerning our oneness with Him, "...that they may be one just as We are one: I in them, and You in Me."

Regardless of whether or not we are conscious of it, without that constant exchange this world as we know it would not even exist..."In Him all things consist." When God set up this whole existence of ours, He put it all in motion with the release of His sound, His Word, "Let there be Light." In the beginning was the Word, and the Word was with God, and the Word was God. He was in the beginning with God. All things were made through

Him, and without Him nothing was made that was made. In Him was life, and the life was the light of men. And the light shines in the darkness, and the darkness did not comprehend (or overcome) it.

John 1:1-5 In the beginning was the Word, and the Word was with God, and the Word was God. The same was in the beginning with God. All things were made by him; and without him was not any thing made that was made. In him was life; and the life was the light of men. And the light shineth in darkness; and the darkness comprehended it not.

Science is only just now catching up with the Word, but what they are discovering these days, especially in the quantum world of physics, is absolutely amazing as it pertains to scripture. He released His sound, His Word out of Eternity and by It all of this that we experience and all that has been experienced in all of history, along with what is to come is held together by It.

Science calls it the zero energy point which is at the very center of the smallest particle. It is what keeps everything from collapsing all around us. Jesus is the fleshly Manifestation of that Word (that upholds all things) He IS the Word. He is the image of the invisible God, the firstborn over all creation.

For by Him all things were created that are in heaven and that are on earth, visible and invisible, whether thrones or dominions or principalities or powers. All things were created through Him and for Him. And He is before all things, and in Him all things consist.

Colossians 1:15-17 Who is the image of the invisible God, the firstborn of every creature: For by him were all things created, that are in heaven, and that are in earth, visible and invisible, whether *they be* thrones, or dominions, or principalities, or powers: all things were created by him, and for him: And he is before all things, and by him all things consist.

I had to look up that word "consist." I've heard this passage misquoted many times I've misquoted this passage myself because of the way I've heard it said as often as "all things exist," rather than "consist." So I looked up the word consist because the Holy Spirit used that word specifically and misquoted it drew my attention to it. The word consist means to be made up or composed, to be comprised or contained, to exist together or be capable of existing together. I found that very interesting all of this is made capable of existing together only in Him. I wanted to lay a scriptural foundation for some of what I wanted to say so that we don't get tripped up by some of the terminology I need to use to help unravel a bit of the mystery of this divine exchange of sound between heaven and earth. This is in order to move into a focus on the coming sounds of worship being released to Heaven by way of intercession, hope, holy anticipation, faith, good works, etc., as well as the sounds of response from heaven to earth in the way of signs and wonders, manifestations, angelic participation, revelation being released, etc. that are coming our way the sounds of Heaven invading earth. There is a sound of breakthrough being released from Heaven in this hour that I believe can even be activated by our sounds of worship mixed with the sound of faith here on the earth. Our agreement with Heaven's agenda will truly affect the outcome.

It may be strange to hear the phrase, "the sound of faith" or "the sound of good works," but energy that is released from these things really does have a sound. Worship is a sound, whether it is audible or inaudible to our natural ear, flowing from us to the Father. When we direct our hearts, our intent toward Him, even when we don't verbalize it, there are waves and/or vibrations that are released into the atmosphere that He sees, smells, hears, tastes—that He receives unto Himself.

Obviously, Scripture uses expression to describe the exchange between God and His creation "Taste and see that the Lord is good." Our prayers are as an incense unto Him and He "fills His nostrils" with it.

But if you were to really look at what is happening at a subatomic level, that unseen realm, our words and sounds are releasing energy into the atmosphere that everything around us is affected by. I had gone through a period of time; I believe several months, where the Lord caused me to see and smell the spirit realm particularly, the realm of emotions. I actually saw the colors and smelled the fragrance that was released from people as they entertained emotions. If a person was angry I saw red coming from them with a foul scent accompanying it. Jealousy in a person released a greenish color, again with a particular foul smell. The most fowl scent of all came with self pity. Demons would see and smell it and flock to the person to fuel the emotion. It worked as well on the flip side of that. Positive emotions released particular colors and pleasant fragrances, causing angels to come. My point is that we see, hear and sense only in part what is taking place in the unseen realm. What we say and what we do does not go unnoticed by God. Every intent; of our heart, every action, every word, every song, it's all "breathed in," so to speak, by God. When a word was released in heaven, with it came music, fragrance, a color of light and a numerical equation.

As I had all these experiences I was so confused. God revealed this revelation and then I thought, "I'm not going crazy after all and I am hearing God on all of this." Something's up in the Spirit and it's a spirit to spirit understanding that He is giving us in this hour. Things have escalated drastically and there is a divine acceleration going on. It is like an earthquake. If you were to say that the end of time as we know it is the center of the quake, then the closer we get to it the stronger and faster the ripples will be that pull us toward it. God is going to be releasing understanding at a greater pace. We are going to be much more accelerated to the unseen realm and I believe we will be more able to sense and discern what is happening there as a result of our actions and our words. We will see and hear more clearly His response and heaven's response, as we become more skilled in the ways of the spirit and the unseen realm. I am setting the stage to move into some explanation of just how our words, our actions, our worship affect the unseen realm. The church is finally exploring that which was meant for us as believers from the beginning of time. We lost the understanding of His ways as we trusted more and more in the thoughts and ways of man... the opinions and traditional way of thinking in Greek based philosophy. We need to begin to pray and ask for the fullness of God to be released in our spirits that we might be enlightened to the way He meant for us to walk with Him even on this earth.

He said He would have those who worship Him in spirit and in truth. There really is something on the horizon in the not so very distant distance. Worship will be the key in releasing much of this. It will be used to change the atmosphere for the Light to penetrate the darkness "and the darkness will not comprehend or overcome it." As He is lifted up He will draw all men unto Him. God is unlocking mysteries and allowing us to peer into things we've not understood until now.

I want to go into the nature of sound and how our words, our intent of heart, impact the atmosphere. The Lord set it all up in the very beginning with the release of the "let there be light" and we are just beginning to catch a glimpse of what that is. We've got to get in touch with the power of our words and, yes, even the intent of our hearts. As we align ourselves with the "sound of heaven" these things will begin to manifest on the earth. I am attempting to introduce the idea that there is a divine exchange going on between heaven and earth at all times.

It's a rather obvious point, yet we go about our daily lives in a state of stupor as to the impact of this truth on us, in us and through us with each breath we take. It is our loss, as well as heaven's loss. It is a great loss to the manifestation of the Kingdom of God on earth. I talked about how God has set up this set of principals and laws in both the seen and unseen realm that everything is subject to.

The laws of the spiritual realm and the physical realm that are intertwined much more than we know. Unfortunately, we've handed over the opening up of these mysteries to science and to the new age philosophers and have lost massive ground over the last 2000 years. In fact, we have gone backwards as we have given ourselves over to the Greek mentality in our approach to God. One impact of that is that we have gone deeper and deeper into our own 'reason', the mind of man, which has taken us farther and farther away from the walk with Him that Adam had in the garden. We have failed to see the fullness of the Cross and the Blood and its impact on the curse of the fall. We have access to so much more than we partake of but that's all about to change. The Hebrew Culture God presented Himself to us through a Hebrew culture. I doubt very much that it was a random choice. The Greek mentality has a strong propensity toward dividing everything up into separate categories; dividing spirit, mind and body. The Hebrew approach is a holistic one, keeping spirit, mind and body as influencing and overlapping each other coming together as a whole. God calls us made in His image. Just as He is 3 in 1 in Father, Son and Holy Spirit, so we are a type of 3 in 1 in mind, body and spirit; yet we are one whole being.

Outside of this truth we will fail miserably in our attempt to understand His ways. Our main concern at this point is in the area of our spiritual endeavors our attempt at communion with God, worshipping Him, and learning of His ways. Back to the Beginning There is that drive within us to get back to what was in His heart in the very beginning. Back to the 'in the Beginning 'when He released the let there be Light 'and there was Light.

The drive to find out what was in His heart in the very beginning when He created us to love and be loved, as companions with Him in the Garden before the mind of man gave entrance to sin by reasoning with the serpent and taking his own way of thinking over God's way. This brings us to where we left off last time with the thought of worshipping Him in spirit and in truth, in the reality of the unseen as well as the perceived realms. We need to gain understanding of these two realms and how they affect our individual lives as well as the advancing of the Kingdom on the earth. A "new sound is coming" is a phrase that you hear everywhere you go. It seems that the Body is in agreement with this phrase, yet no one really knows what that means. I'm not saying I know what it means, either, but I want to address at least a few aspects of that sound as I see it. I believe it is a sound of faith... a sound of understanding... and the sound, of the overcomer. It is also a combination of our sounds and the reality sounds of the supernatural, combined into one sound that carries the authority of heaven in it a supernatural sound that should be natural for us by now, but is not.

However it is soon coming and there are those who have at least attempted to attune their ear to it. It's a difficult process because we've not been given the tools, but Truth is coming. The mind of man and our reasoning's, will give way to it. God said, "come, let us reason together", not "you guys figure it out in your own thoughts and get back to Me." That's pretty much been our approach ever since we let Constantine set our course down the Greek path of reasoning. The Sound of a Shift Saints are saying this more and more "you heard that, too, didn't you." They took comfort in the fact that others had heard it, and it filled them with anticipation of something coming. When we hear a sound like that it causes a shift in us. Depending on just how much of it we allow into our being, it can literally cause a shift in us. It can introduce something into our fiber that until that point was not there... or perhaps it was, but is only now being awakened. The sound of truth or deception can cause a shift in us if we embrace it, but it's not just mental or spiritual, it is physical also. Sound travels by way of vibrations that are transported from molecule to molecule on what is called waves.

The energy that is created mixes with our energy. We are made up primarily of energy when you get down to the subatomic levels of things. It's amazing that we actually look like empty space for the most part, but that empty space is actually energy. I realize this is simplified, but the point I'm making is that we constantly emit and receive energy. We impact everything and everything impacts us. We can control that a bit, but I won't go into that quite yet because it would take us off the path too far. There is a very interesting study done on water and the affect sound, music or words. You might wonder what that has to do with us as humans, but we are 70% water as adults.

It shows the impact positive and negative words have on water. Even different styles of music affect the water for good or bad. Again, it's an energy thing. Interestingly enough the words "love and gratitude" were of the most positive impact. Prayer was released consistently for 3 days over a polluted lake and at the end of three days the water was pure. Granted, the people praying were of varying faiths and beliefs but it's a spiritual principal that was set up in the beginning when God formed this existence of ours. There are spiritual and physical laws that have been put into motion by Him that we have not even begun to tap into. The same is true of plants. Studies have been done that show plants "reacting" to music. Classical music stimulates growth and even shows plants growing toward the music, wrapping itself around the speakers. Hard rock music causes some plants to be stunted in their growth, some to grow away from the music and some to even die. It's the energy of the sound waves that are affecting the plants. Thank God we are finally beginning to wake up and take back the truths and look into the mysteries of creation! I've heard it said many times that the New Agers have stolen the things of God. They didn't steal anything we gave it over to them by not exercising our dominion over the earth as the Sons of God. We abandoned the truths of the spirit and took up the mind of man, what we could see and touch and hear with our natural senses. It's time for the Sons of God to come into their inheritance of the mysteries of creation, both in spirit and in truth.

He, Who Has Ears to Hear, Let Him Hear

Sound is a profound thing when understood and utilized in its fullness. Mankind has barely begun to realize the effect it has on our body, mind, and spirit.

During the days of the harvest we must grasp the implications of sound relative to the triune nature of man. The scripture records the Lord oftentimes saying "He who has ears to hear, let him hear."

This clearly implies that we can have ears, yet not hear. (Matthew 11:15, 13:9, 13:43, Mark 4:9, 4:23, 7:16, Luke 8:8 and 14:35.)

It's a statement made to highlight a point, much like "Truly, truly I say to you." That particular line of thought is taken even further in Romans 11:8 saying, just as it is written, God has given them a spirit of stupor, eyes that they should not see, and ears that they should not hear, to this very day. During this day's religion, God at times even closes our ears to what is being said. It needs to be a conscious prayer of ours that He would open our ears to what the Spirit is saying in this hour. Just like it takes God to love God, it takes God to hear God. We would be wise to ask Him to do that in us. The Act of Hearing It is reported that our own minds can close our ears to certain sound frequencies. If fact, if you have been exposed to someone who constantly says things to you that you don't want to hear, things that criticize you, your ear will stop itself from ingesting, so to speak, the frequency levels of that person's voice. It could affect your hearing the rest of your life. Fortunately, they are now coming up with treatment to repair the damage.

It's just something a person does to survive the sound that is causing death in them. That is why it is so important what we speak over our children. There are numerous studies being conducted today involving sound and vibration and it's affect on us. Organs can be affected positively or negatively by sound; yes, even music.

The Spirit has been showing me some very interesting things about our hearing that we need to be aware of. Many times Paul warned the saints about what they listened to that would lead them astray. We are approaching the day that "Even the very elect would be fooled "if God did not intervene. Now, I'm not trying to scare you, but I feel like we need to be educated in some of these things to make the most of what God gave us to use. We often hear that "the new sound" or "the sound of heaven" is about to be released. What if we don't have ears to hear it? Actually, our ear is much more than something we hear with. When a fetus is in the womb the ear is the first sensory organ to be fully developed and there is a reason for that. When sound enters the ear, it goes through an amazing technical process that actually turns it into electrical impulses which charge the brain. In a fetus, this charge actually causes the brain to grow as early as 4 $^{1}/2$ months. There is a muscle that is activated at this point inside the ear that never rests until you die. This is the only muscle in the entire body that this is true of. We literally "absorb" sound non stop until the day we die, the mechanics of hearing. There is a cranial nerve attached to both sides of the eardrum that extends throughout the body and is attached to every organ except the spleen.

To some extent, what we hear with our ears affects every organ in our body. We not only hear by sound being transferred through the air, but also through our skin and bones. Our entire body takes in sound in one way or another. Jeremiah declared, His word was in my heart like a burning fire shut up in my bones. I was weary of holding it back and I could not.

Jeremiah 20:9 Then I said, I will not make mention of him, nor speak any more in his name. But *his word* was in mine heart as a burning fire shut up in my bones, and I was weary with forbearing, and I could not *stay.*

There is a spiritual and natural implication to this verse. The sound of God's word had entered his bones and he was compelled to let it out. Have you ever felt like that? I certainly have, especially during time of intense worship. This truth can give us even greater understanding of Ezekiel's vision of the dry bones.

Ezekiel 37:4 Again he said unto me, Prophesy upon these bones, and say unto them, 0 ye dry bones, hear the word of the LORD.

He is commanding the bones to hear a sound a particular sound that they might live. Is that "the sound" that is being released today? A sound that causes spiritually dry bones to come together and produce life! It is interesting that the bones are dry because water is one of the most effective conductors of sound.

A pregnant woman can communicate with their child because the child is in a sack of water in the womb; the water outside the womb was most effective. Natural and Spiritual as it is in the natural, so it is in the spirit. The words we listen to and the sounds we allow to wash over us, affect us in diverse ways.

Jeremiah 6:10 To whom shall I speak, and give warning, that they may hear? behold, their ear *is* uncircumcised, and they cannot hearken: behold, the word of the LORD is unto them a reproach; they have no delight in it. If we do not have God's Spirit flourishing in us, our ears remain uncircumcised; Jeremiah says they cannot heed. It's not that we just choose not to, it's not possible. We can have uncircumcised hearts as well as ears. We must learn to hear what the Spirit is saying in this hour, particularly in a day when we are given the warning that even the very elect would be fooled apart from the Lord's intervention.

Lord, please cause our hearts and ears to be circumcised that we may hear with understanding, your sounds! What is our Sound? Sound is measured by vibratory frequencies. Science has discovered that we all vibrate at a certain frequency. They are presently determining how to take the frequency of an individual and convert it to audible sound. There is actually music that each of us carries within our being at sound frequencies that are inaudible to the natural ear, but are sensed by those around us even by creation itself. Do we resonate with His Truth? Do we echo the sound of the Spirit? Perhaps, the more of Him that resonates in us causes us to "sound" just like Him and become one with Him. These are all things to ponder as we attempt to hear the sound that is being released today in this "divine exchange" between heaven and earth.

This realization is only going to increase... "He that has ears to hear, let him hear what the Spirit is saying."

SUPERNATURAL POWER

In many ways, Daniel and his three friends provide a representation of the manner in which the Lord will equip his people for the special assignments set before us.

The Babylonian captivity of natural Israel provides a prophetic portrait of our condition and the Lord's promise for deliverance of spiritual Israel. Daniel describes the special empowerment from heaven imparted to these loyal young men. God gave them, intelligence in every branch of literature and wisdom; Daniel even understood all kinds of visions and dreams.

Daniel 1:17 As for these four children, God gave them knowledge and skill in all learning and wisdom: and Daniel had understanding in all visions and dreams.

The Lord gave them by inspiration, revelatory knowledge and intelligence in various matters of writing and literature. The Lord quickened in them special skills to apprehend and articulate spiritual understanding and heavenly wisdom. Daniel was notably gifted with supernatural perception into all manner of visions and dreams. There was a specific impartation from God that empowered them to excel in the apprehension of wisdom and governmental scholarship. The Lord bestowed by spiritual transference the blessing of unique knowledge and exceptional capacity in literature and all manner of written work. This pattern will also be followed in this day when the Lord discovers devoted hearts of obedience and loyalty.

There are vast storehouses of revelatory insight and supernatural knowledge involving the Scriptures, creation, science, the arts and many other subjects that will be entrusted to saints who follow the model established by Daniel and his three friends.

A PROPHETIC STANDARD

These four young men provide a prophetic standard for the spiritually strong who know their God and carry out great exploits. They will intimately know God and engage the revelatory realm of heaven. In them will be an excellent spirit granting acute perception and understanding to interpret dreams and visions, clarify revelatory experiences and solve difficult and mysterious problems. They will be people who apprehend insight from the throne room and respond to the invitation to "come up here" to be shown things to take place in the future. A few years ago during a prophetic experience, the Lord specifically stated to me that Daniel 1:17 was spiritually linked to Ephesians 1:17.

These are parallel passages stating the same promise from different time frames. One is from the old covenant outlining the dealings of God during difficult times but also pointing to a future day of supernatural intervention into the lives of mankind. The other is expressed in the new covenant recording for all generations the heritage of the saints. Despite our perceived personal limitations or lack of educational opportunities, the Lord is a quickening Spirit. He has promised to give life to our mortal bodies with His Spirit and grant to us the Spirit of Revelation that will access mysteries, secrets and revelatory knowledge as our legacy in Him.

TOKENS OF THE PAST

Many who attended Maria Woodworth-Etter meetings at the turn of the 20th century would be caught up in the Spirit to experience visions and revelations of the Lord. Some would be commissioned in their encounter as missionaries to foreign lands and emerge from their visionary revelation capable of fluently speaking the language of the nation to which they were called. It is the Father's good pleasure to reveal to us the kingdom and perform awesome deeds that only He can achieve. It was a small thing for Him to rejuvenate the bodies of Abraham and Sarah and quicken them with strengthening virtue. Even after Sarah's death and well over one hundred years of age, Abraham continued in the strength imparted to him and bore many more sons. The Lord is more than able to equip us to access the unfathomable treasures hidden in Him that require supernatural gifts like those entrusted of the apostle Paul. As the Bible also clearly promises, the Holy Spirit knows what is hidden in darkness and reveals the deep and secret things. Light dwells with Him bringing illumination to that which has been set apart and reserved for the generation of destiny.

Daniel 2:22 He revealeth the deep and secret things: he knoweth what *is* in the darkness, and the light dwelleth with him.

Even now there are individuals engaging the revelatory realm of heaven receiving downloads of insight into physics, light, sound and spiritual colors. (You can read more about this in another book, "A Greater Anointing."

The visitation of the apostle John to the throne room of heaven was both visual and audible. His experience disclosed awesome sights, sounds and vibrant colors surrounding the Lord's seat of dominion and victory. The more understanding we have of that realm the greater our ability to cooperate with heaven in the demonstration of the kingdom dominion on the earth. Those being awakened to this realm and seeking understanding into science, physics and the elements of creation are not super geniuses with great scientific minds. Most are ordinary Christians who are tapping into the heart of God desiring to release supernatural endowments of His mind into the Bride. Much is going to be spoken and written in the coming days involving this dimension of our heritage.

Like Einstein, an insatiable desire to understand creation and the Creator will flourish in the hearts of many Christians. Access to the spiritual books of heaven will be granted providing divine wisdom, revelatory knowledge and supernatural strategy.

LIVING IN THE SUPERNATURAL

In this Chapter I will outline real keys for developing living in the supernatural and a greater sensitivity to the Spirit of God. First you'll learn how to be a conqueror in the battle for the mind, heart, and emotions and how to use your authority strategically in this struggle. You'll be encouraged as you realize that winning this fight ultimately means that you've won a prize of great, great value possessing the mind of Christ. And you'll come to appreciate why having God's mind is absolutely essential to living in the supernatural every day. At the end I'll share how to have the eyes of your understanding opened so that you can see beyond this physical world. So, if your spiritual eyes are testing out at less than 20/20, then this Chapter will certainly help to improve your vision! God wants us to develop a supernatural way of living! I'm so contending for this supernatural standard of living and I'm pushing through for you hungry ones who wants this just as much as I do. It's a lifestyle beyond just having prophetic encounters and experiences here and there. I'm talking about raising the bar to the level where you are in the spirit daily and that's the norm! It's so obviously supernatural, and yet it's as natural as breathing. So my goal in this Chapter is to lay a foundation that will help you open the way for the Spirit to lead you every day. I'll outline some real keys, practical keys, for developing a greater sensitivity to the Holy Spirit and then I'm going to teach about being spiritually minded and about the battle in the mind, heart and emotions. You'll be equipped to overcome what hinders you from operating in the mind of Christ!

THE BATTLE FOR THE MIND, HEART AND EMOTIONS

The first thing we all need to overcome to live this way is our mind. I came to understand that ultimately what is far better than just my own mind is having the mind of Christ. However, there are battles that go on in the mind. One is what I call the warfare of the mind. It's the spiritual warfare that goes on in our mind and thoughts, and the torment of the mind. I'm talking about the battle, the worry, the distraction in the thought life, as well as the things that go on in the demonic realm to control the mind and prevent us from entering into the mind of Christ. And the battle to overcome doesn't end there! We also need to overcome distractions in our hearts and emotions because there are things that go on in the heart or emotional realm that can also keep us from entering into the realm of spirit. So let's take a look at what it takes to overcome the battle in our minds and clear the air, so to speak, so that we can experience the mind of Christ.

First of all, I want to explain that the heart, mind, and understanding are all one in the same.

For instance when the apostle Paul spoke to the Ephesian church about having the eyes of their understanding opened, it was in the context of this oneness.

Ephesians 1:18 The eyes of your understanding being enlightened; that ye may know what is the hope of his calling, and what the riches of the glory of his inheritance in the saints,

Secondly, in orderto have the eyes ofourunderstanding opened, or have an eye to see in the invisible realm, we need to walk in peace. Because when there is anxiety, stress and worry it fuels spiritual warfare in the mind and it disrupts our peace so that we miss getting to the place we want to be in the spirit. Therefore it is imperative to have a peace on our minds and hearts so that we can begin to operate in the spirit of the mind and enter into a greater dimension in the realm of the spirit

Ephesians 4:23 And be renewed in the spirit of your mind;

Proverbs 4:23 Keep thy heart with all diligence; for out of it *are* the issues of life.

We need to determine within ourselves to make a choice. Choose to "let the peace of God rule in your hearts..."

Colossians 3:15 And let the peace of God rule in your hearts, to the which also ye are called in one body; and be ye thankful.

Are we going to let the peace of God rule our hearts and minds? Or are we going to choose the disruption? Are we going to be overcome by what is going on in the thought realm? Because the warfare that goes in those areas is the greatest strategy of the enemy to keep us out of the realm of the supernatural dreams, visions, angels, hearing the voice of God, prophetic experiences, glory and open heavens it's that simple.

We need to choose to cast down arguments and every high thing that exalts itself against the knowledge of God, bringing every thought captive to the obedience of Christ.

2 Corinthians 10:5 Casting down imaginations, and every high thing that exalteth itself against the knowledge of God, and bringing into captivity every thought to the obedience of Christ;

I have found the greatest key for me over the years to really enter into the realm of the spirit is when I take captive every demonic arrow, thought, argument, every high thing that exalts itself, and every whispering demonic voice from the accuser. I still my mind, emptying out all the junk; I overcome in my mind and think about myself the way that God thinks and I get the victory. But it is a choice! And it is your choice! If we can learn to begin to guard our hearts and let the peace of God rule in our hearts and if we can find victory in our emotions and in our thoughts, then we will have an open door daily to the realm of the supernatural.

In fact for us today, more than ever before, there is an open heaven, an increase of the word of the Lord and revelation!

UNDERSTAND THE OPPOSITION

Yes, God is giving the spirit of wisdom and revelation and the knowledge of Him like never before and the knowledge of the glory of the Lord covering the earth as the waters cover the sea.

Habakkuk 2:14 For the earth shall be filled with the knowledge of the glory of the LORD, as the waters cover the sea.

Much in the spirit is available to us! There's more for us than the nine manifestations/gifts of the Spirit, as vital as they are.

1 Corinthians 12:7-11 But the manifestation of the Spirit is given to every man to profit withal. For to one is given by the Spirit the word of wisdom; to another the word of knowledge by the same Spirit; To another faith by the same Spirit; to another the gifts of healing by the same Spirit; To another the working of miracles; to another prophecy; to another discerning of spirits; to another *divers* kinds of tongues; to another the

interpretation of tongues: But all these worketh that one and the selfsame Spirit, dividing to every man severally as he will.

No wonder there is such opposition from the enemy coming against the church. The devil doesn't want the church today to truly experience the glory, the riches of God's glory. Witchcraft and mind control, even a demonic assignment has come against the mind of Christ in the church today so that we can't receive what God has for us. It manifests like a cap, a spiritual cap, a spiritual ceiling or a hood that's made the prophets, especially the seer prophets, blind.

It's an outside and external battle from a demonic mob that has one assignment: keeping believers from believing, living in, and experiencing the supernatural.

This attack is aimed directly against the church walking in and having the mind of Christ. Think about that. Remember that today, more than ever, many believers are actually having deeper and deeper revelation about Jesus. With this revelation, naturally they have the mind of Christ in a greater way! Now what could be more disturbing to the enemy than a whole lot of believers who think the way God thinks? So don't miss this: We actually have an ability to think the way that God thinks; to see, to feel, the way that God does. All the wisdom of God, all the knowledge of God, all the understanding of God, it's all the mind of Christ! The Apostle Paul said that we have the mind of Christ! Since we have the mind of Christ then we have the knowledge, the wisdom, the understanding, and what God thinks! And yet, when you look around at the church today, are we really operating in the mind of Christ? No we're not. Nevertheless, the potential is there!

Having the mind of Christ means that we actually have the ability to step into the very way that God thinks. The very creative process of God, the very knowledge of God in every situation and every decision that you make in life, the mind of Christ can actually come upon you as an anointing.

You can think, speak, and act the very way that Christ thought, spoke, and acted. How many of you would like to walk in that God inspired realm? You can, if you learn how to be spiritually minded and if you overcome in the thoughts, heart, and emotions. Then you will possess the mind of Christ. Yes, there may be moments when you are in the supernatural, but I am talking about living in the supernatural in a much greater way by overcoming some of the warfare that goes on in our thought life.

RESIST THE TEMPTATION TO JUDGE CARNALLY

As a matter of fact, the warfare in our thought life can manifest in such tricky ways.

Now I want to ask a question. How many men and women in the church today are prevented from entering into the presence of the Lord and experiencing all that

He has because of a judgment, a criticism, or an attitude in the heart?

We need to guard the heart and the mind with peace. You know, there will always be a test. There will always be something that will offend our minds; in fact, so sufficiently, that we may decide to turn our backs on something that God actually intended us to pursue. Think about that. A lot is at stake because for those who represent the very thing that you and I want a deeper prayer life, more anointing, etc. it's all too easy to have an attitude, even an arrogance and a competitive spirit toward them. That ungodly mind set will not only hinder us from learning from the Holy Spirit, it will stop us from learning from the vessel He is flowing through (such as a Christian teacher, leader, mentor, friend), and it will wreck our ability to experience the supernatural or live a supernatural lifestyle. So we need to check our heart.

I want to explain why having your spiritual sight fully engaged and activated is absolutely essential to living in the supernatural. When you discover why it's not God's will for you to be spiritually "visually impaired" you'll be stirred to walk in strong faith as I bring you outstanding examples that explain how to live in the supernatural. As well you'll come into a clear understanding about some of the pitfalls to watch out for that can keep you from a supernatural standard of living making carnal judgments, walking in sin, and more.

What's the opposite of being led by the Spirit of God? It's groping around blindly in the dark within the carnal mind. But fumbling around leaning on our own understanding, lacking spiritual sight, is not God's plan for us. So then, what is spiritual sight all about?

SPIRITUAL VISION IS NORMAL AND NATURAL

Although you sense there is more for you in life, even healing for your blindness, you don't know any other way to live so you just go on learning how to live with this difficult handicap. Now close your eyes and walk around for a few minutes, after picking a safe place to do so, and imagine that you are blind. I did this in a meeting once that was full. You can just imagine the results of this test. How did being blind affect you? Did you wonder if you would stumble over any obstacles in your path? Were you disoriented? Did you have any idea where you were going? For the purpose of this test, your answers to those four questions connect directly to the experience of those believers who try to live the Christian life wanting to be led by the Holy Spirit and sensing that God has much more for them yet they're stumbling around not entering into the fullness because their spiritual eyes or spiritual sight are not activated. I hope that, like me, you can conclude from our little experiment that lacking spiritual eyesight is a real handicap. Why? Because this hinders believers from being led by the Holy Spirit into the fullness of what God has for them. Now, what does that fullness involve?

We actually need our spiritual eyes working the eyes of our heart or the eyes of our understanding so that we can see more, perceive more, and discern more, spiritually. More means that we see beyond what our natural eyes are revealing to us. And what lies beyond is the invisible spiritual realm wherein we sense: the leading of God, His still small voice, the angelic presence, the great cloud of witnesses, and much more. This is the supernatural realm. So it's understandable that spiritual vision is absolutely essential if we are going to walk in the supernatural realm, living a supernatural lifestyle. Yet for many of us in the church today, it's like there are scales on our eyes blinding us from really seeing. Well, those scales need to fall off! And they will if we press into God's heart and receive revelation about what it truly means to see fully with the eyes of our understanding. Seeing beyond our physical world and seeing in the invisible realm ought to be normal and natural! Think about that; 20/20 spiritual vision has always been at the heart of God's plan for us. After all, 20/20 vision is normal vision! Having the eyes of our hearts activated with full spiritual vision, in reality, is not something unique or unusual!

Are the leaders of today's Church seeing clearly? It seems that too many ministries are blind.

God Wants Your Spiritual Sight Activated

But why is it that so many in the church today seem content staying blind or satisfied settling for "visual impairment"? I want to answer that question by asking another question! Do you think that Jesus Christ just wanted to heal the physical problem of blindness? Look at this. When He was in His hometown, Nazareth,

He preached in His synagogue, reading the prophetic writing scribed by the prophet Isaiah.

Luke 4:18 The Spirit of the Lord *is* upon me, because he hath anointed me to preach the gospel to the poor; he hath sent me to heal the brokenhearted, to preach deliverance to the captives, and recovering of sight to the blind, to set at liberty them that are bruised,

We only have to read a few chapters about Jesus and His Ministry to realize that healing the physical part of blindness wasn't His sole intention. Jesus wanted the people to receive full recovery to both their spiritual and their physical sight. Since you are reading this text that means you already have physical sight. But there's more. Today God wants you to know that the time is ripe to push through for total sight full recovery, full restoration! God wants your spiritual sight totally engaged and activated! Truly, those scales will fall off by way of more revelation from Him.

FULLY LOADED

So let's begin receiving further revelation by asking ourselves two more questions! Where are our spiritual eyes? How do we see?

You can see with all five of your senses. Ponder that. Not just one way to see! God created us fully loaded to see!

Hebrews 5:14 But strong meat belongeth to them that are of full age, *even* those who by reason of use have their senses exercised to discern both good and evil.

2 Timothy 2:15 Study to shew thyself approved unto God, a workman that needeth not to be ashamed, rightly dividing the word of truth.

I've come to understand that when certain manifestations happen, no matter how subtle they might appear to be, they have a meaning that needs to be discerned and heeded. In my experience most often when I have an encounter it goes on in the same area of my brain that I daydream; that same creative place where I can just close my eyes and reach into my "data base" of memories and trigger a memory. (It's not visualization.) To further explain: at times when we smell something, it's like that smell will take us back to a memory and we're "there" again, we can feel it; because God has placed something in us, in our minds that are very creative.

This is the realm where dreams, trances and many prophetic experiences take place. That realm is in the mind, and it's the eye or heart of our understanding or the spiritual eye too.

THE MIND OF CHRIST

1 Corinthians 2:16 For who hath known the mind of the Lord, that he may instruct him? But we have the mind of Christ.

Psalms 16:7 I will bless the LORD, who hath given me counsel: my reins also instruct me in the night seasons.

Would like to have access to that realm, with your mind, heart and inmost being operating? After all, we are instructed to set our mind and our affections on things above, not on things on earth.

Colossians 3:2 Set your affection on things above, not on things on the earth.

You see, only when our affections, our emotions, our mind, and our thoughts are set on things above can the peace of God truly come; and it's a guard.

Remember last week I said that we need to let the peace of God rule; it guards our hearts and minds. Then the door of the spirit realm opens up and we begin to live in the supernatural realm because there is a direct connection between peace, the mind, and having our hearts set on entering into the realm of the Spirit. Set your affections on things above. Yet also let's not forget that the heart or the inner person needs to be clean.

PURITY IS REQUIRED

Our purity of heart will always eventually come to a crucial testing point. We may want the eyes of our understanding opened, but there is a price to pay in the area of purity if we want to live a holy, true supernatural way of living. Sometimes after God tests the quality of the purity in our hearts, depending on what He finds, He will allow a blindness to come over the prophets and seers, which manifests like a covering or a hood that comes over their heads.

Isaiah 29:10 For the LORD hath poured out upon you the spirit of deep sleep, and hath closed your eyes: the prophets and your rulers, the seers hath he covered.

Could it be that one of the reasons for this action is because of some kind of sin?

Isaiah 29:13-15 Wherefore the Lord said, Forasmuch as this people draw near *me* with their mouth, and with their lips do honour me, but have removed their heart far from me, and their fear toward me is taught by the precept of men: Therefore, behold, I will proceed to do a marvellous work among this people, *even* a marvellous work and a wonder: for the wisdom of their wise *men* shall perish, and the understanding of their prudent *men* shall be hid. Woe unto them that seek deep to hide their counsel from the LORD, and their works are in the dark, and they say, Who seeth us? and who knoweth us?

Remember, I said that witchcraft, mind control, and demonic assignments come against the mind of Christ in the church so that we can't receive what God has for us. The fact is sin opens the door for the enemy; but we can close that door. At times I've seen in the spirit (in our meetings) that some of the people there actually have a hood over their head that acts like a cover, just as the above scripture verse explains. Perhaps that's you, and your prophetic seer gifting is not functioning.

JESUS DIDN'T JUDGE BY APPEARANCE

God wants us to have a true supernatural impartation for more dreams, more visions, more encounters, and living in the supernatural daily. But once again, we need to have the right heart attitude for this to happen or we could really miss it.

You know, mindsets coming from judgment, criticism, and negative attitudes can completely derail us from receiving from the Holy Spirit or the anointed person that He is flowing through. So I want to challenge you, concerning this issue. God doesn't want us to be sidelined and we need to resist the ungodly temptation to judge carnally by appearance. Remember the words of the prophet Isaiah about Jesus:

Isaiah 11:3, 4 And shall make him of quick understanding in the fear of the LORD: and he shall not judge after the sight of his eyes, neither reprove after the hearing of his ears: But with righteousness shall he judge the poor, and reprove with equity for the meek of the earth: and he shall smite the earth with the rod of his mouth, and with the breath of his lips shall he slay the wicked.

PRAYER IS NEEDED

I've realized that I need to pray first and take authority over whatever demonic mob may want to resist and block me so that it could be pushed out of the way, and then I could safely go into heaven.

I want to emphasize the importance of prayer in connection with any encounters in the supernatural realm. Of course this applies to living in the supernatural too, because to really live in the supernatural is to live a life of prayer, a life of intimacy with our Father, with the Lord Jesus Christ, and with the Holy Spirit. Also please don't miss this: Jesus Christ is the only door to every heavenly encounter "I am the door of the sheep...1 am the door. If anyone enters by Me, he will be saved, and will go in and out and find pasture..."

John 10:7 Then said Jesus unto them again, Verily, verily, I say unto you, I am the door of the sheep.

John 10:9 I am the door: by me if any man enter in, he shall be saved, and shall go in and out, and find pasture.

SEATED WITH CHRIST

To be seated with Christ in heavenly places signifies the delegation of authority.

Through the process of redemption we are given a divine opportunity to share in the kingdom rule of the Lord and entrusted with a realm of authority signified by the "seat" or place of dominion. Naturally, that designation is not randomly given to an infant in the faith without having grown in the stature of Christ. That is not to say this position is in anyway earned or merited.

Rather, it is to signify a place of growth and maturity evident from the work of the Holy Spirit. This process molds us into the image of Christ making us capable of maintaining this spiritual position, without corrupting or prostituting its great spiritual value. Those who overcome are granted permission to sit with him on His Throne as he overcame to sit with the Father.

There is a process of triumphing over spiritual deception and resistance that must be attained in order to qualify for this high office. It is by grace that it is provided to the Bride of Christ. Yielding to the work of grace positions the Bride to share in His nature and qualify for this heavenly position. Put plainly, it is not a position that we flippantly approach by merely walking the isle of the church and reciting a prayer. It is by individuals encountering the Lord of Glory and being changed from glory to glory into His image. From this place of union and fellowship, the overcomers are seated and granted dominion and authority to rule with Him. This is an ancient issue that goes back to the original rebellion of Satan and his desire to be seated with God to rule and reign. What Satan could not obtain through pride and rebellion, the Lord is freely offering to us by virtue of His sacrificial offering and work of redemption.

We are presently living in the transition from the Church age into the manifestation of kingdom reality. There is a tremendous display of truth coming as manna for this day to transform and prepare a body of people to fully engage the kingdom realm of heaven and manifest that reality in the earth. Even during the dark ages when the written word was inaccessible to the masses, the Living Word manifested Himself to those who were genuinely seeking Him from a pure heart with right motives. Many historical accounts are recorded to validate this reality. The apostle Paul was granted a great privilege to be a messenger in his day to present the Bread of Life to his generation.

As a reward for that place of leadership and sacrifice, he is given the honor of presenting the overcomers" of his day to the Lord as a pure virgin. He said,

2 Corinthians 11:2 For I am jealous over you with godly jealousy: for I have espoused you to one husband, that I may present *you as* a chaste virgin to Christ.

That same privilege is given to the messengers of each generation charged with the commission and mandate to present the manna of the day to the people of God.

There are messengers sent to each age with a divine mandate and deposit of truth that is like a fire locked up in their bones that must be expressed and demonstrated. These are the stars in the hand of the Lord to present the revelation of heaven to the church. This present day has been identified with the promise of an unprecedented release of heavenly manna through many messengers to groom a people to bear the likeness and nature of Christ. It will be a multiplication of the light given throughout the seven church ages.

Isaiah 30:26 Moreover the light of the moon shall be as the light of the sun, and the light of the sun shall be sevenfold, as the light of seven days, in the day that the LORD bindeth up the breach of his people, and healeth the stroke of their wound.

This future bride could not be just an ordinary woman she had to be of the same heritage and lineage as Isaac became bone of his bone and flesh of his flesh. This is the perfect typical scenario to be executed in this day as well.

There is emerging to be the loyal and faithful servants who are trustworthy stewards of the mysteries and power of God to secure a radiant and passionate bride for the Lord. Daniel was shown the great deposit of mysteries to be unfolded in the days identified as the "end-time" but was not allowed to articulate the revelation that he saw. Rather, it was reserved along with the eminent secrets that John observed and was required to seal.

Daniel 12:4 But thou, 0 Daniel, shut up the words, and seal the book, *even* to the time of the end: many shall run to and fro, and knowledge shall be increased.

Revelations 10:4 And when the seven thunders had uttered their voices, I was about to write: and I heard a voice from heaven saying unto me, Seal up those things which the seven thunders uttered, and write them not.

The manna is described in the Scriptures as the bread of angels. It is associated with the provision of heaven for the children of Israel as they wandered in the wilderness of Sinai. It was the perfect sustenance providing all that they needed. There was not one feeble or sick among them while they shared in this bread from heaven. God spoke this to me; it was a symbolic representation of the Person who would identify Himself as the Bread who has come from Heaven providing all that we need. Yes I believe it is for provision and a sign from God. Those who eat of this bread shall live forever without difficulty or weakness. This is further verified in stating that man shall not live by bread alone but by every Word that proceeds from the mouth of God. It is not an optional duty but a mandated responsibility by the grace of God to be identified with those who overcome and share in the blessings and rewards of the victorious ones.

The revelation of His Word is the bread from heaven. It is the perfect manna that will absolutely sustain us in perfection. Throughout each church age portions of the heavenly manna was delegated.

The early apostles were entrusted with great revelation and insight into Kingdom mysteries and a segment of the people embraced that revelation. However, compromise entered the corporate body in with an organizational spirit that severed the free flow of manna from heaven. Only small measures of the bread of Life came for years until the promises of Joel were remembered by the Lord.

Joel 2:25 And I will restore to you the years that the locust hath eaten, the cankerworm, and the caterpiller, and the palmerworm, my great army which I sent among you.

The process of progressive restoration began with the great reformation. We are now standing on the threshold of the generation long foreseen by the prophets and patriarchs throughout the ages. The saints of this day will not only be granted access to the manna of Heaven and divine mysteries, but also the grace to apprehend and experience the reality. This will be the generation to whom the Lord comes by placing His foot on the land and the sea, clothed in a rainbow with the open book in His hand. For many generations the book has been sealed but the end-time generation has the unimaginable promise of living in the day in which the Lord Himself will break the seals. It is His promise to give the now open book to His chosen ones to be eaten and consumed by a generation hungry for the reality of heaven.

REALITY OF ANGELS

The Church has a hard time believing that Angels exist. I'm going to back up with scripture that they are real and we can be in contact and even converse with angels. The one thing I want to point out is we never worship angels.

Psalms 91:11 For he shall give his angels charge over thee, to keep thee in all thy ways.

Hebrews 13:2 Be not forgetful to entertain strangers: for thereby some have entertained angels unawares.

Angels are mentioned in the Old Testament 108 times. The word Angel or Angels appear in the books of the Law, writings of Moses 32 times.

What are Angels? Who are they? Angels are created spirit beings.

Psalms 148:2-5 Praise ye him, all his angels: praise ye him, all his hosts. Praise ye him, sun and moon: praise him, all ye stars of light. Praise him, ye heavens of heavens, and ye waters that *be* above the heavens. Let them praise the name of the LORD: for he commanded, and they were created.

Hebrews 1:14 Are they not all ministering spirits, sent forth to minister for them who shall be heirs of salvation?

Another good definition of Angels comes through Greek & Hebrew words.

Angel means: Messenger

Angel delivers messages to God's men and women. Angels

are immortal.

Luke 20:36 Neither can they die any more: for they are equal unto the angels; and are the children of God, being the children of the resurrection.

Angels never get sick and never die.

OUT RANKING MAN

Psalms 8:5 For thou hast made him a little lower than the angels, and hast crowned him with glory and honour.

2 Peter 2:11 Whereas angels, which are greater in power and might, bring not railing accusation against them before the Lord.

Lucifer tried to rule but failed and one day, in Heaven we shall even judge the Angels.

1 Corinthians 6:3 Know ye not that we shall judge angels? how much more things that pertain to this life?

ANGELS ARE INTELLIGENT

2 Samuel 14:20 To fetch about this form of speech hath thy servant Joab done this thing: and my lord *is* wise, according to the wisdom of an angel of God, to know all *things* that *are* in the earth.

ANGELS ARE HOLY

Mark 8:38 Whosoever therefore shall be ashamed of me and of my words in this adulterous and sinful generation; of him also shall the Son of man be ashamed, when he cometh in the glory of his Father with the holy angels.

ANGELS ARE INNUMERABLE.

Hebrews 12:22 But ye are come unto mount Sion, and unto the city of the living God, the heavenly Jerusalem, and to an innumerable company of angels,

Innumerable means you cannot count them.

Job 25:3 Is there any number of his armies? and upon whom doth not his light arise?

ANGELS ARE STRONG

2 Thessalonians 1:7 And to you who are troubled rest with us, when the Lord Jesus shall be revealed from heaven with his mighty angels,

Psalms 103:20 Bless the LORD, ye his angels, that excel in strength, that do his commandments, hearkening unto the voice of his word.

Angels are invisible. It is rare to see angels.

Numbers 22:22-31 And God's anger was kindled because he went: and the angel of the LORD stood in the way for an adversary against him. Now he was riding upon his ass, and his two servants *were* with him. And the ass saw the angel of the LORD standing in the way, and his sword drawn in his hand: and the ass turned aside out of the way, and went into the field: and Balaam smote the ass, to turn her into the way. But the angel of the LORD stood in a path of the vineyards, a wall *being* on this side, and a wall on that side. And when the ass saw the angel of the LORD, she thrust herself unto the wall, and crushed Balaam's foot against the wall: and he smote her again. And the angel of the LORD went further, and stood in a narrow place, where *was* no way to turn either to the right hand or to the left. And when the ass saw the angel of the LORD, she fell down under Balaam: and Balaam's anger was kindled, and he smote the ass with a staff. And the LORD opened the mouth of the ass, and she said unto Balaam, What have I done unto thee, that thou hast smitten me these three times?

And Balaam said unto the ass, Because thou hast mocked me: I would there were a sword in mine hand, for now would I kill thee. And the ass said unto Balaam, *Am* not I thine ass, upon which thou hast ridden ever since *I was* thine unto this day? was I ever wont to do so unto thee? And he said, Nay. Then the LORD opened the eyes of Balaam, and he saw the angel of the LORD standing in the way, and his sword drawn in his hand: and he bowed down his head, and fell flat on his face.

WE ARE NEVER TO WORSHIP ANGELS

Revelations 22:8, 9 And I John saw these things, and heard *them.* And when I had heard and seen, I fell down to worship before the feet of the angel which shewed me these things. Then saith he unto me, See *thou do it* not: for I am thy fellowservant, and of thy brethren the prophets, and of them which keep the sayings of this book: worship God.

The bible declares not only are we not to worship angels, but also they don't want to be worshiped.

Colossians 2:18 Let no man beguile you of your reward in a voluntary humility and worshipping of angels, intruding into those things which he hath not seen, vainly puffed up by his fleshly mind,

This is just the beginning of "The Reality of Angels."

OPEN HEAVENS

A chosen generation, that's us! We have been chosen for such a time as this.

1 Peter 2:9 But ye *are* a chosen generation, a royal priesthood, an holy nation, a peculiar people; that ye should shew forth the praises of him who hath called you out of darkness into his marvellous light:

We're a royal priesthood, said the Apostle Peter, special people, sanctified, to display the virtues of Christ. So let's set our hearts on fulfilling that great call the display that demonstrates both God's kingdom and His power on earth as it is in heaven!

HEAVEN ON EARTH

Then, as heaven manifests in the natural realm, both the rule and the reign of Jesus Christ will be known in the earth. "Let God be glorified!"

Yet, don't miss this: The key to bringing that manifestation to earth is an open heaven a portal through which the kingdom of God invades the earth! Perhaps one of the best biblical examples to illustrate this kingdom invasion is when the heavens opened over Jesus while He was baptized (by John the Baptist). God's kingdom invaded the earth in the form of a dove the Spirit of God that rested upon Jesus

Luke 3:21, 22 Now when all the people were baptized, it came to pass, that Jesus also being baptized, and praying, the heaven was opened, And the Holy Ghost descended in a bodily shape like a dove upon him, and a voice came from heaven, which said, Thou art my beloved Son; in thee I am well pleased.

He was empowered (anointed) for ministry. God anointed Him with the Holy Spirit and with power! And immediately, living under that open heaven, "then Jesus, being filled with the Holy Spirit, was led by the Spirit into the wilderness" for forty days

Luke 4:1-13 And Jesus being full of the Holy Ghost returned from Jordan, and was led by the Spirit into the wilderness, Being forty days tempted of the devil. And in those days he did eat nothing: and when they were ended, he afterward hungered. And the devil said unto him, If thou be the Son of God, command this stone that it be made bread. And Jesus answered him, saying, It is written, That man shall not live by bread alone, but by every word of God. And the devil, taking him up into an high mountain, shewed unto him all the kingdoms of the world in a moment of time. And the devil said unto him, All this power will I give thee, and the glory of them: for that is delivered unto me; and to whomsoever I will I give it. If thou therefore wilt worship me, all shall be thine. And Jesus answered and said unto him, Get thee behind me, Satan: for it is written, Thou shalt worship the Lord thy God, and him only shalt thou serve.

(9) And he brought him to Jerusalem, and set him on a pinnacle of the temple, and said unto him, If thou be the Son of God, cast thyself down from hence: For it is written, He shall give his angels charge over thee, to keep thee: And in *their* hands they shall bear thee up, lest at any time thou dash thy foot against a stone. And Jesus answering said unto him, It is said, Thou shalt not tempt the Lord thy God. And when the devil had ended all the temptation, he departed from him for a season.

Because the heavens were open, He functioned in a different "arena." In other words, His mind was in heaven. Living in the fullness of heaven's realities, Jesus carried the substance of heaven in His ministry in the virtue, in the rule, in the reign, in the dimension of "as it is in heaven," Now through miracles, healings, salvations deliverance, signs and wonders. Wow, Lord!

EXPERIENCES & REVELATIONS

In fact, Jesus lived and ministered in that spiritual atmosphere 24/7. We need to make that our goal too, because under an open heaven the spiritual atmosphere is ripe for prophetic experiences, and those encounters greatly influence both our level of anointing and our determination for fulfilling the purposes of God.

Revelations 4:1 After this I looked, and, behold, a door *was* opened in heaven: and the first voice which I heard *was* as it were of a trumpet talking with me; which said, Come up hither, and I will shew thee things which must be hereafter.

Although the invitation to "come up here" was to one person; specifically, John, I believe God is saying, "I'm now releasing in a greater corporate dimension, the experience.

Revelations 19:11-21 And I saw heaven opened, and behold a white horse; and he that sat upon him *was* called Faithful and True, and in righteousness he doth judge and make war. His eyes *were* as a flame of fire, and on his head *were* many crowns; and he had a name written, that no man knew, but he himself. And he *was* clothed with a vesture dipped in blood: and his name is called The Word of God. And the armies *which were* in heaven followed him upon white horses, clothed in fine linen, white and clean. And out of his mouth goeth a sharp sword, that with it he should smite the nations: and he shall rule them with a rod of iron: and he treadeth the winepress of the fierceness and wrath of Almighty God. And he hath on *his* vesture and on his thigh a name written, KING OF KINGS, AND LORD OF LORDS. And I saw an angel standing in the sun; and he cried with a loud voice, saying to all the fowls that fly in the midst of heaven, Come and gather yourselves together unto the supper of the great God; That ye may eat the flesh of kings, and the flesh of captains, and the flesh of mighty men, and the flesh of horses, and of them that sit on them, and the flesh of all *men, both* free and bond, both small and great. And I saw the beast, and the kings of the earth, and their armies, gathered together to make war against him that sat on the horse, and against his army. And the beast was taken, and with him the false prophet that wrought miracles before him, with which he deceived them that had received the mark of the beast, and them that worshipped his image. These both were cast alive into a lake of fire burning with brimstone. And the remnant were slain with the sword of him that sat upon the horse, which *sword* proceeded out of his mouth: and all the fowls were filled with their flesh.

When the heavens open over us, we'll begin to have visions and dreams, visitations of the Lord, and revelations. We'll begin to see in the spirit and we'll begin to minister under the power and the authority of an open heaven, bringing the manifestation of Jesus Christ in His glory with power, miracles, healing, signs and wonders.

WELCOME THE OPEN HEAVENS

I believe there is a "place" where there is an invitation for each and every one of us to pray for spiritual understanding, for the eyes of our hearts to be opened, and for us to be filled with the spirit of wisdom and revelation. It's an atmosphere where we can make ourselves available to receive solid teaching and guidelines from God's word to help us exercise our spiritual senses. Also, it's where we can learn to open and sanctify our imagination, and begin to have the eyes of our understanding enlightened, whereby we begin to touch the dimension of seeing the dimension of visions, trances, dreams, and angelic visitation. One reason is because the "dimension of seeing" goes hand in hand with the seer anointing, and God wants to give us that anointing. God is emphasizing Revelation Chapter 4, verse 1, opening it up, issuing an invitation into the throne the third heaven and into the anointing represented in that particular scripture. There's been a real emphasis in the last 10 years or so on the prophetic "you can all prophesy one by one, that all may learn and all may be encouraged" that's edification and exhortation. It's good, but the open heavens dimension is different from the prophetic dimension. Many believers, as prophetic people, seem content if they can just hear God and prophesy once in a while. Their attitude is: I don't need visions, trances, dreams and angelic visitations. I don't need that stuff, Brother. I walk by faith. I got the word, and that's enough for me. Whether or not I see or feel anything, I'm going to believe God. Well, I walk by faith too. By faith I know I have access to come boldly before God's throne, to ask Him to let me see the throne. Then, with expectation I begin to press in for throne room (third heaven) experiences. It's like this about such experiences: If I don't ask and if I don't have an expectation, it won't happen.

I've come to the place in my relationship, passion, and intimacy with Jesus where I believe that God wants me to see, hear, feel, and experience with my spiritual senses

I want to challenge some of you. It's time to overcome the fear of being deceived and come to grips with the fact that God in His ability to keep you is greater than the devil's ability to deceive you.

CERTAIN PLACES

Open heavens occur over certain geographical areas that are marked by God. For example Jacob experienced an open heaven at a place which he named Bethel.

Genesis 28:1-7 And Isaac called Jacob, and blessed him, and charged him, and said unto him, Thou shalt not take a wife of the daughters of Canaan. Arise, go to Padanaram, to the house of Bethuel thy mother's father; and take thee a wife from thence of the daughters of Laban thy mother's brother. And God Almighty bless thee, and make thee fruitful, and multiply thee, that thou mayest be a multitude of people; And give thee the blessing of Abraham, to thee, and to thy seed with thee; that thou mayest inherit the land wherein thou art a stranger, which God gave unto Abraham. And Isaac sent away Jacob: and he went to Padanaram unto Laban, son of Bethuel the Syrian, the brother of Rebekah, Jacob's and Esau's mother. When Esau saw that Isaac had blessed Jacob, and sent him away to Padanaram, to take him a wife from thence; and that as he blessed him he gave him a charge, saying, Thou shalt not take a wife of the daughters of Canaan; And that Jacob obeyed his father and his mother, and was gone to Padanaram;

This is where he had an amazing dream about a ladder that stretched from earth to heaven with angels ascending and descending on it. Some places, because of their spiritual history, are noted to be locations where people will often experience an open heaven. In fact, there are places where the heavens are open more than in other places.

Most of you are familiar with previous moves of God in places such as Toronto (The Toronto Blessing), the meetings in Pensacola, and Lakeland, just to name a few. Just like in Jacob's day, today, there are certain places where heaven is open, geographical locations where you are more likely to have an encounter with God. I know that everyone's walk with the Lord is unique. For some of you, the whole aspect of open heavens is unfamiliar. For others, you've recognized moments under an open heaven, wanting more.

YOU ARE MADE FOR THIS!

Yes, you can! You are made for this! Look. It's in the Bible. It's God's idea. Just take a look at what the Apostle Paul said:

Colossians 3:1, 2 If ye then be risen with Christ, seek those things which are above, where Christ sitteth on the right hand of God. Set your affection on things above, not on things on the earth.

Receive that truth, since it's by your determination to set your mind "on high" like this, that you will know God.

Ephesians 1:17 That the God of our Lord Jesus Christ, the Father of glory, may give unto you the spirit of wisdom and revelation in the knowledge of him:

That's what Paul prayed; it's for us too! Then, with that heavenly mindset you'll be in the right position to advance the Kingdom of God in the earth! Now for those who still might be skeptical, here's a question: Why would Paul pray that God would give that to us if He didn't want us to have wisdom and revelation and the knowledge of Him, which only comes out from encountering, tasting and seeing Him? Paul also prayed since the people were Christians, but they weren't living in the experience of heavenly revelation that the eyes of their understanding be enlightened; that they would know the hope of His calling and the riches of the glory of His inheritance.

Ephesians 1:18 The eyes of your understanding being enlightened; that ye may know what is the hope of his calling, and what the riches of the glory of his inheritance in the saints,

EXERCISE SPIRITUAL SENSES

That prayer (Eph. 1:18) is just as alive today as it was back then, for the Ephesians. Today, God wants our understanding to be enlightened!

2 Corinthians 4:18 While we look not at the things which are seen, but at the things which are not seen: for the things which are seen *are* temporal; but the things which are not seen *are* eternal.

We're being encouraged by God to look there, to the things which are not seen yet, also consider this there's nothing better than living under an open heaven for seeing the unseen! But we live in the temporal world, and we're all too comfortable with what we see, feel and hear in the natural.

Yes, we have good natural senses, but God says, "I want you to set your eyes on these things which are not seen, I want you to look for them, because the things which are seen are temporary, but there's an unseen realm, and that realm is eternal."

We need to begin to exercise our spiritual senses and become more conscious of that realm.

ALLOW THE HOLY SPIRIT TO TEACH YOU

The Bible from the beginning to the end is full of the supernatural, the reality of the supernatural normal men like you and me, having extraordinary encounters with God. There was Elijah, taken into heaven in a chariot.

2 Kings 2:11 And it came to pass, as they still went on, and talked, that, behold, *there appeared* a chariot of fire, and horses of fire, and parted them both asunder; and Elijah went up by a whirlwind into heaven.

There was Paul, who had an abundance of visions and revelations.

2 Corinthians 12:1 It is not expedient for me doubtless to glory. I will come to visions and revelations of the Lord.

2 Corinthians 12:7 And lest I should be exalted above measure through the abundance of the revelations, there was given to me a thorn in the flesh, the messenger of Satan to buffet me, lest I should be exalted above measure.

In fact, he couldn't even talk about those things because it would be unlawful for him to talk about them.

2 Corinthians 12:2-4 I knew a man in Christ above fourteen years ago, (whether in the body, I cannot tell; or whether out of the body, I cannot tell: God knoweth;) such an one caught up to the third heaven. And I knew such a man, (whether in the body, or out of the body, I cannot tell: God knoweth;) How that he was caught up into paradise, and heard unspeakable words, which it is not lawful for a man to utter.

Peter went into a trance, and what came out of that encounter transformed the entire early church.

Acts 10:9, 10 On the morrow, as they went on their journey, and drew nigh unto the city, Peter went up upon the housetop to pray about the sixth hour: And he became very hungry, and would have eaten: but while they made ready, he fell into a trance,

Just read the incredible experiences of John, the revelator, in the Book of Revelations and then there was Elisha.

1 Kings 19:16-21 And Jehu the son of Nimshi shalt thou anoint *to be* king over Israel: and Elisha the son of Shaphat of Abelmeholah shalt thou anoint *to be* prophet in thy room. And it shall come to pass, *that* him that escapeth the sword of Hazael shall Jehu slay: and him that escapeth from the sword of Jehu shall Elisha slay. Yet I have left *me* seven thousand in Israel, all the knees which have not bowed unto Baal, and every mouth which hath not kissed him. So he departed thence, and found Elisha the son of Shaphat, who *was* plowing *with* twelve yoke *of oxen* before him, and he with the twelfth: and Elijah passed by him, and cast his mantle upon him. And he left the oxen, and ran after Elijah, and said, Let me, I pray thee, kiss my father and my mother, and *then* I will follow thee. And he said unto him, Go back again: for what have I done to thee? And he returned back from him, and took a yoke of oxen, and slew them, and boiled their flesh with the instruments of the oxen, and gave unto the people, and they did eat. Then he arose, and went after Elijah, and ministered unto him.

2 Kings 2:1-25 And it came to pass, when the LORD would take up Elijah into heaven by a whirlwind, that Elijah went with Elisha from Gilgal. And Elijah said unto Elisha, Tarry here, I pray thee; for the LORD hath sent me to Bethel. And Elisha said *unto him, As* the LORD liveth, and *as* thy soul liveth, I will not leave thee. So they went down to Bethel. And the sons of the prophets that *were* at Bethel came forth to Elisha, and said unto him, Knowest thou that the LORD will take away thy master from thy head to day? And he said, Yea, I know *it;* hold ye your peace. And Elijah said unto him, Elisha, tarry

here, I pray thee; for the LORD hath sent me to Jericho. And he said, *As* the LORD liveth, and *as* thy soul liveth, I will not leave thee. So they came to Jericho.

And the sons of the prophets that *were* at Jericho came to Elisha, and said unto him, Knowest thou that the LORD will take away thy master from thy head to day? And he answered, Yea, I know *it;* hold ye your peace. And Elijah said unto him, Tarry, I pray thee, here; for the LORD hath sent me to Jordan. And he said, *As* the LORD liveth, and *as* thy soul liveth, I will not leave thee. And they two went on. And fifty men of the sons of the prophets went, and stood to view afar off: and they two stood by Jordan. And Elijah took his mantle, and wrapped *it* together, and smote the waters, and they were divided hither and thither, so that they two went over on dry ground. And it came to pass, when they were gone over, that Elijah said unto Elisha, Ask what I shall do for thee, before I be taken away from thee. And Elisha said, I pray thee, let a double portion of thy spirit be upon me. And he said, Thou hast asked a hard thing: *nevertheless,* if thou see me *when I am* taken from thee, it shall be so unto thee; but if not, it shall not be *so.* And it came to pass, as they still went on, and talked, that, behold, *there appeared* a chariot of fire, and horses of fire, and parted them both asunder; and Elijah went up by a whirlwind into heaven. And Elisha saw *it,* and he cried, My father, my father, the chariot of Israel, and the horsemen thereof. And he saw him no more: and he took hold of his own clothes, and rent them in two pieces. He took up also the mantle of Elijah that fell from him, and went back, and stood by the bank of Jordan; And he took the mantle of Elijah that fell from him, and smote the waters, and said, Where *is* the LORD God of Elijah? and when he also had smitten the waters, they parted hither and thither: and Elisha went over. And when the sons of the prophets which *were* to view at Jericho saw him, they said, The spirit of Elijah doth rest on Elisha. And they came to meet him, and bowed themselves to the ground before him. And they said unto him, Behold now, there be with thy servants fifty strong men; let them go, we pray thee, and seek thy master: lest peradventure the Spirit of the LORD hath taken him up, and cast him upon some mountain, or into some valley. And he said, Ye shall not send. And when they urged him till he was ashamed, he said, Send. They sent therefore fifty men; and they sought three days, but found him not. And when they came again to him, (for he tarried at Jericho,) he said unto them, Did I not say unto you, Go not? And the men of the city said unto Elisha, Behold, I pray thee, the situation of this city *is* pleasant, as my lord seeth: but the water *is* naught, and the ground barren. And he said, Bring me a new cruse, and put salt therein. And they brought *it* to him. And he went forth unto the spring of the waters, and cast the salt in there, and said, Thus saith the LORD, I have healed these waters; there shall not be from thence any more death or barren *land.* So the waters were healed unto this day, according to the saying of Elisha which he spake. And he went up from thence unto Bethel: and as he was going up by the way, there came forth little children out of the city, and mocked him, and said unto him, Go up, thou bald head; go up, thou bald head. And he turned back, and looked on them, and cursed them in the name of the LORD. And there came forth two she bears out of the wood, and tare forty and two children of them. And he went from thence to mount Carmel, and from thence he returned to Samaria.

Allow the Holy Spirit to teach you about the unseen realm. Set your mind on things above. Sanctify Your Imagination

Just like an eagle flies way up high, and with his keen eyesight he sees far off into the distance, God wants you to be high "by setting your mind on things above," and to have eagle eyes clear prophetic vision that sees far off. However, the first thing you must do is sanctify your imagination. If you're going to have eagle eyes you need to sanctify the eyes of your understanding by guarding what you do with your natural eyes. After all, you and we are joint heirs, members of the body of Christ, and if we're really a chosen generation, if we're really a royal priesthood, set to display the virtues of Christ then we have to live like it. Sanctified! God wants a royal priesthood, and that priesthood is called royal only because it is holy.

Proverbs 20:27 The spirit of man *is* the candle of the LORD, searching all the inward parts of the belly.

Yes, the spirit of a man is the lamp of the Lord that's how God brings revelation. Revelation, it's in your soul and it's in your spirit, God as a lamp.

Psalms 119:105 Thy word *is* a lamp unto my feet, and a light unto my path.

He brings revelation and communicates with you in the realm of your imagination on the inside in the same place where you think, have fantasies, good or bad. So you must be careful about which things you allow into your eye-gates, the things that you watch, because they affect your soul your mind, will and emotions.

Ephesians 4:22-24 That ye put off concerning the former conversation the old man, which is corrupt according to the deceitful lusts; And be renewed in the spirit of your mind; And that ye put on the new man, which after God is created in righteousness and true holiness.

He told them not to walk like the Gentiles their minds were confused and full of darkness. They were immoral.

Ephesians 4:17-19 This I say therefore, and testify in the Lord, that ye henceforth walk not as other Gentiles walk, in the vanity of their mind, Having the understanding darkened, being alienated from the life of God through the ignorance that is in them, because of the blindness of their heart: Who being past feeling have given themselves over unto lasciviousness, to work all uncleanness with greediness.

He told them not just to live holy lives, but he also warned them that if they didn't, if they were immoral, impure, or greedy, they would not have an inheritance in the Kingdom of Christ and God. Just like the Ephesians, we need to take Paul's words to heart. We must honor God by living pure lives. Purity is a sign of respect that reflects the high value we place on our vast, rich inheritance in Christ Jesus. Part of our inheritance, one big chunk that God wants to give us, is a well developed, sanctified seer anointing. So press in to God and honor Him by receiving all of the inheritance that He wants to give you now. Today is the season of the Lord's favor and the hour of His visitation! Capture it. Be fully engaged, completely renewed, ready to ride the wave of His greater glory into this season.

HEAVEN IS REAL

In this enlightening Chapter entitled, Heaven is real, I'll show how God's whole kingdom, both the heavenly realm and the earthly realm, work together to manifest heaven on earth. First I'll establish an important foundational principle concerning the purpose for learning about heaven's realities.

Heaven's realities are heavenly and earth's realities are of the earth different yet just watch what happens when they converge! You'll see the fullness of God's kingdom, and it's a supernatural one, at work in the earth "on earth as it is in heaven."

Matthew 6:10 Thy kingdom come. Thy will be done in earth, as *it is* in heaven.

When I think about Heaven and Earth; understands their partnership (revelation) and by learning to walk in that supernatural realm (demonstration), you'll defy human logic because both revelation and demonstration only come by the Spirit of God! Now having said that, you might think this is all pretty heavy stuff! I want to ground this Chapter by emphasizing the purpose for learning about heaven's realities as well as the purpose for walking in the supernatural. Both are meant to glorify God His goodness and His redemptive love so that the lost would come into right relationship with Him. May this truth help us to block any improper motives from creeping in, including pride, as we mature in our ability to demonstrate the reality of God's supernatural kingdom? Now we're ready to jump into heaven's realities!

HEAVEN & EARTH PARTNER HOW REAL IS HEAVEN?

Wow! Heaven's realities became visible, manifesting on the earth financial blessings, people encouraged, gold teeth and because of that "wonder" a man made a decision for Jesus Christ. Still, even with this evidence, I want to challenge you. "How real is heaven? Can we really go into the invisible realm, change something in the invisible, and then see it show up in the natural realm?"

HEAVEN BECOMING REAL IN THE EARTH

I say we can change things, and the reason why we can is all because of God. His faithfulness! His desire to teach us by giving us revelation! By a revelation I got the offering in the spirit realm (in the invisible) but it was birthed, first, by God's rhema word to me.

Romans 4:17 (As it is written, I have made thee a father of many nations,) before him whom he believed, *even* God, who quickeneth the dead, and calleth those things which be not as though they were.

God calls those things into existence that don't exist in the visible realm. He calls them forth and speaks them into existence as if they already are, because they are in heaven, in the eternal purpose of God in eternity in the real world. Remember, heaven is real. In heaven, they already are. There's already a true copy. For example, Moses was divinely instructed when he was about to make the tabernacle. God told him to "make all things according to the pattern shown to him on the mountain,"

Hebrews 8:5 Who serve unto the example and shadow of heavenly things, as Moses was admonished of God when he was about to make the tabernacle: for, See, saith he, *that* thou make all things according to the pattern shewed to thee in the mount.

David was given the pattern for the Temple that his son Solomon would build.

1 Chronicles 28:11-19 Then David gave to Solomon his son the pattern of the porch, and of the houses thereof, and of the treasuries thereof, and of the upper chambers thereof, and of the inner parlours thereof, and of the place of the mercy seat, And the pattern of all that he had by the spirit, of the courts of the house of the LORD, and of all the chambers round about, of the treasuries of the house of God, and of the treasuries of the dedicated things: Also for the courses of the priests

and the Levites, and for all the work of the service of the house of the LORD, and for all the vessels of service in the house of the LORD. *He gave* of gold by weight for *things* of gold, for all instruments of all manner of service; *silver also* for all instruments of silver by weight, for all instruments of every kind of service: Even the weight for the candlesticks of gold, and for their lamps of gold, by weight for every candlestick, and for the lamps thereof: and for the candlesticks of silver by weight, *both* for the candlestick, and *also* for the lamps thereof, according to the use of every candlestick. And by weight *he gave* gold for the tables of shewbread, for every table; and *likewise* silver for the tables of silver: Also pure gold for the fleshhooks, and the bowls, and the cups: and for the golden basons *he gave gold* by weight for every bason; and *likewise silver* by weight for every bason of silver: And for the altar of incense refined gold by weight; and gold for the pattern of the chariot of the cherubims, that spread out *their wings,* and covered the ark of the covenant of the LORD. All *this, said David,* the LORD made me understand in writing by *his* hand upon me, *even* all the works of this pattern.

The blueprints existed already in heaven. Once we learn how to partner with God by seeing whatever He directs us to see in the heavens in the invisible realm touch it, and see it in the heavens and once we learn how to speak with authority in that realm, then it manifests here on the earth.

What you do in that kind of experience will change what happens to you in this realm. Everything hinges on God! I say that because it's God's idea to open up heaven's realities (the supernatural) to us. Not only does God see fit to open up the supernatural to us, He does it in a natural way. Spending close times with the Lord, taking His word seriously, and being open to the supernatural made the difference. The same goes for you! If you want to experience the reality of the heavenly realm, then be open to it, get close to God in your walk with Him, and honor Him. As you do, you'll be in the right position for God to teach you about the supernatural; and in a natural way He'll take you into heavenly experiences. The key is divine revelation. God speaks to you, and you believe what He tells you it might be in a vision, a trance, a dream, or something else and you allow it. It's not, "name it and claim it," or let's have a bunch of visions, or let's have a bunch of dreams.

And always remember, the purpose for walking in heaven's realities is to glorify God so that the lost would come into right relationship with Him. He is mighty to save!

DIVINE INTERVENTION

Faith at work through praise and worship brings heaven to earth we're talking about a real world on earth as it is in heaven heaven's realities! Certainly, God wants His will to be done on earth as it is in heaven! He wants to partner with us and show us what's going on in heaven, heaven's realities, so that they will be real on the earth, too. I tell you, when your partnership with God is at a level where you can co-labor with Him so that heaven and earth converge, your whole life in Christ will take on a whole new meaning.

We have a big, big God. He wants us to live our lives "out of the box" just like He does! How is the world going to know who He is if we don't look like Him!

What captures the world's attention witchcraft in books and movies, drugs and perversion, to name just a few will continue if God doesn't get His chance to put on a big display about Himself through Christians a whole lot more than how it's currently happening! We need to get with it! We need to find out what God wants us to do and really do it! Take Moses. In his day the magicians had power, occult power. Had Moses failed to recognize and walk in God's power, had he just tried to take on Pharaoh and his magicians with a "let's try and take a good stab at it" attitude, would the might of God's glory been seen? Would the fear of God come? Remember, God told Moses to tell Pharaoh that He was going to display His power so that the whole nation of Egypt would see that there was no other God like Him, that His fame would spread throughout the earth.

Exodus 9:14 For I will at this time send all my plagues upon thine heart, and upon thy servants, and upon thy people; that thou mayest know that *there is* none like me in all the earth.

Exodus 9:16 And in very deed for this *cause* have I raised thee up, for to shew *in* thee my power; and that my name may be declared throughout all the earth.

How is the world going to see God's power and majesty, how will nations be won to Christ unless we that's you and that's me get serious and boldly demonstrate who He really is? If this Chapter is grabbing your heart, then today, I want you to "take it to the Lord." Maybe you need to get on our knees and get serious with God. The hour demands it! The days are evil! God needs you, and He needs me, fully equipped and ready for action!

ENGAGING THE REVELATORY REALM

When we engage the revelatory realm of Heaven, it carries us into a supernatural dimension of faith in which miracles, signs and wonders result.

The healing expression of the 1940s and '50s introduced a more pronounced Kingdom ministry from the revelatory realm that opened the heavens for a season of healing and miracles unprecedented in church history. During that time, many souls came into the Kingdom and Truth was restored. On May 7, 1946 a dear man by the name of William Branham went to a secret place of prayer, deep in the woods of Indiana. This man of God had been experiencing supernatural encounters for which neither he nor his fellow ministers had a grid or base of understanding to compare. Finally, in desperation, he retreated to the secluded place, determined to discover from the Lord what these things were and their significance. According to his testimony, something supernatural occurred well into the night and deep into his heartfelt time of prayer, a Heavenly Light entered the room in which he was praying. The supernatural light appeared as a pillar of fire and projected illumination in much the same way that a spotlight would. At that moment he heard footsteps walking toward him and eventually standing under the beam of light. One can only imagine the frightful reaction of someone alone, deep in a wooded area without electricity encountering a supernatural being walking into the room in a real and tangible way. The angelic messenger's audible salutation was similar to those we discover in the Scriptures.

He said, "fear not, for I am sent from the Presence of Almighty God." As soon as Brother Branham heard this voice, he recognized it as the one who had spoken to him many times throughout his life. The messenger continued by saying that he was sent to impart a commission of divine healing to that generation. However, there was an additional and unique aspect of the commission that introduced a fresh dimension of the revelatory realm of Heaven that accompanied the tremendous healing ministry. A supernatural gift was imparted to allow this man to detect by revelation the specific illnesses, demonic oppressions and deadly diseases that oppressed the people. He was further instructed that if he walked humbly in this gift, he would, at some point, be allowed to discern the very thoughts and intents of the heart. This commissioning introduced an amplified expression of the omniscient attributes of the Lord.

(Omniscient Means: having complete or unlimited knowledge, awareness, or understanding; perceiving all things)

When the supernatural revelation was released, it carried the faith of the people above the realm of doubt and unbelief, into the realm of faith where miracles are accessed. On June 14, 1946 the first public healing meeting under this commissioning took place in St. Louis, MO. The impact and responses were immediate. The miracles began to occur on a mass scale that many writers of that day determined were unprecedented in modern church history. When the second phase of the commission was executed, the minister would stand before the people and communicate by revelation their name, illness, resident address, past events, private prayers and many other detailed secrets that no one knew except them and the Lord. Witnesses testify that this produced such tangible faith in the corporate meetings that the feeling prevailed that anything was possible in such an atmosphere of the anointing.

The Implications for our day with something of that magnitude occurring in just the prior generation, we are compelled to ask the question, what is the significance of this type of ministry for our generation? It is our devoted belief that this form of ministry was a pioneering work of the Spirit to introduce to our generation the fashion in which the revelatory realm of Heaven can be accessed to release supernatural faith. His was a forerunner ministry. The things that occurred between 1946 and 1956 were much more than just a revival. It was the beginning of the end time ministry that initiated the fulfillment of prophetic Scriptures pointing to this generation. Like Moses, these signs were given so that the people would believe.

Exodus 4:8 And it shall come to pass, if they will not believe thee, neither hearken to the voice of the first sign, that they will believe the voice of the latter sign.

According to the commission given to Moses, these supernatural signs have a "voice." There is a message that accompanies the signs. The message is one of restoration of the covenant people of God to a place of spiritual prominence and submission to the lordship of Jesus Christ. It was much more than a gift of the Spirit. It was the manifestation of the Person of the Word discerning the thoughts and intents of the heart.

Hebrews 4:12, 13 For the word of God *is* quick, and powerful, and sharper than any twoedged sword, piercing even to the dividing asunder of soul and spirit, and of the joints and marrow, and *is* a discerner of the thoughts and intents of the heart. Neither is there any creature that is not manifest in his sight: but all things *are* naked and opened unto the eyes of him with whom we have to do.

The Living Word discerns and peers directly into the secret corridors of our lives. All things are open and lay bare before the eyes of Him with whom we have to do. When the Spirit of the Lord manifests in a tangible way, it brings forth revelation, not merely as a "word of knowledge," but the "Spirit of knowledge and revelation" flowing to the benefit of God's people. It carries the reassuring virtue that God not only knows about us individually, but cares and is willing to give expression to the understanding of His heart. The Spirit of the

Lord is upon me, the commission to be imparted to this generation is discovered in,

Luke 4:18 The Spirit of the Lord *is* upon me, because he hath anointed me to preach the gospel to the poor; he hath sent me to heal the brokenhearted, to preach deliverance to the captives, and recovering of sight to the blind, to set at liberty them that are bruised,

The Spirit of the Lord coming upon a: consecrated and prepared body of people to release counsel and might; wisdom & revelation; knowledge & the reverent fear of God.

Luke 4:18, 19 The Spirit of the Lord *is* upon me, because he hath anointed me to preach the gospel to the poor; he hath sent me to heal the brokenhearted, to preach deliverance to the captives, and recovering of sight to the blind, to set at liberty them that are bruised, To preach the acceptable year of the Lord.

That is the Kingdom reality that rested upon the Lord and the one that was restored in 1946. It is far more than just a ministry or the exercise of spiritual gifts. It is His Divine Presence: The Spirit of the Lord is coming upon His body to do the same works that He did while on the earth in human form. The greatest gift is to be able to step aside so that He can step in and do through us the same things that He did. That is what was introduced to us through the prior generation and the incredible demonstration of Kingdom power and authority witnessed in that day. There were a few who touched that realm as spiritual spies who introduced it to the present generation of destiny. Many of the ministers of the prior generation, who flowed in realms of power as healing evangelists, were devoted and sincere saints of God. They approached the Lord in simplicity and humility and obtained from Him the anointing needed to carry the gospel of salvation and power to an entire generation. Even so, the prior generation did not enter into the fullness of the mandate nor sustain the unveiling of the Kingdom message.

If such a tragedy can happen to them, how much more to us in this day! We need the great grace of God to access and sustain the open heaven needed to fulfill the harvest generation.

Joshua 1:2 Moses my servant is dead; now therefore arise, go over this Jordan, thou, and all this people, unto the land which I do give to them, *even* to the children of Israel.

Joshua 1:5 There shall not any man be able to stand before thee all the days of thy life: as I was with Moses, *so* I will be with thee: I will not fail thee, nor forsake thee.

Although Joshua was anointed with the same Spirit that rested upon Moses, his ministry to the people had little similarity of its application. There was no need for Joshua to write the law. Moses already accomplished that. The Spirit that rested upon Moses and was imparted to Joshua, unveiled an additional aspect of the Lord as the Warrior who displaced the giants take over of a place in the land promised to God's covenant people.

The scribe of the Kingdom brings forth from his treasure both things old and new. While we examine the prior expression of His manifested Presence, we must also remain open to the unprecedented demonstrations of the Spirit. Eye has not seen and ear has not heard nor has it yet entered into the heart of man all that will be revealed through the mind of Christ in this day. We only know that it will be tremendous and require eyes & ears opened to the revelatory realm of Heaven and a wholly submitted spirit, soul and body.

THIRD HEAVENS

As I have pointed out in numerous teachings, I believe this generation is on the threshold of experiencing a spiritual restoration that will equate in its prominence with the recovery of the Jewish people to the land of Israel.

The Scriptures referring to this day and the various signs of the times explicitly point to this reality. Isaiah foresaw the natural and spiritual restoration and announced:

Isaiah 49:8-10 Thus saith the LORD, In an acceptable time have I heard thee, and in a day of salvation have I helped thee: and I will preserve thee, and give thee for a covenant of the people, to establish the earth, to cause to inherit the desolate heritages; That thou mayest say to the prisoners, Go forth; to them that *are* in darkness, Shew yourselves. They shall feed in the ways, and their pastures *shall be* in all high places. They shall not hunger nor thirst; neither shall the heat nor sun smite them: for he that hath mercy on them shall lead them, even by the springs of water shall he guide them.

The apostolic reformationwill ignite the reestablishment of the Church to function in genuine spiritual power and authority. From that identity, even greater places in God await. These will include the unfolding of the Priesthood and the appropriate Biblical apprehension of son-ship through overcomers who have discovered rest in God and His rest in them.

Hebrews 4:8, 9 For if Jesus had given them rest, then would he not afterward have spoken of another day. There remaineth therefore a rest to the people of God.

The apostle Paul was entrusted with notable understanding involving the strategy of the Holy Spirit in leading the Church. His epistles clearly outline the many offices established in God's government along with various gifts and the impartation of visions and revelations. He likewise demonstrated powerful teachings that came by the revelation of Jesus Christ, and affirmed the messages with power. All of this, and more, will be fully operating in the days ahead. Many saints will be given the opportunity to experience God in ways articulated by Paul, John and the notable patriarchs of old. The Biblical prophecies pointing to the end time generation highlight a people who will be anointed with the Holy Spirit, to witness numerous things through visions, dreams and spiritual encounters.

Many will also be taken into the Third Heaven, and like Paul, experience realms in God impossible to communicate. The Lord is introducing Himself in a fresh and profound way. Revelation of His Attributes One of the most captivating principles in walking with God is the revelation of His many glorious attributes.

It has always been fascinating to discover through the Scriptures, the diverse reactions of the Lord's servants when He manifested Himself to them.

For instance, following the Lord's death, burial and resurrection, He appeared to His bewildered disciples as a loving Friend. Luke 24 highlights this wonderful encounter. The disciples were gathered in an upper room behind closed doors, as two excited disciples shared their supernatural encounter on the road. While these things were being shared, the Lord Himself stepped into their midst with a salutation of peace and friendship. Very quickly, their startled reaction turned to joy as he encouraged them saying,

Luke 24:38, 39 And he said unto them, Why are ye troubled? and why do thoughts arise in your hearts? Behold my hands and my feet, that it is I myself: handle me, and see; for a spirit hath not flesh and bones, as ye see me have.

This loving revelation of His attribute as the Friend and Master penetrated their hearts of His disciples with an eternal bond of affection and loyalty. The Lord demonstrated His ability to appear in such a way that His followers are not overwhelmed by the sheer power of His presence. This revelation of Him as Friend disclosed one attribute of His great character and forever altered His disciples. On the other hand, the beloved disciple John, the very one who once laid his head upon the breast of God, also encountered this same Christ, but with the revelation of a different portion of His attributes. In Revelations 1, we discover the Lord Jesus manifesting Himself to John as the Great Judge. So overwhelming was this experience that when John saw the Lord he, "fell at His feet like a dead man." That was the reaction of the aged apostle when beholding the revelation of Jesus as the Just Judge. The same Person...only different manifestations of His attributes, which produced an entirely different response. This same pattern can be discovered throughout Scripture. The celebrated prophet Moses was able to establish a face to face relationship with the Lord and spoke with Him as a friend speaks to his friend. I cannot think of a more extravagant honor to any man. Even so, the Lord further introduced Himself before Israel in such virtue and overwhelming demonstrations of His creative power, that it placed even the heart of Moses in great fear. The purpose for drawing this conclusion is to discover that the reaction is varied but always powerful and awe-inspiring. In this day, we are being offered an open door to the realm of the Spirit that is truly exceptional in its excellence. Moreover, it is one that must be administered with solemn care and reverence. The Lord is showing us that His people must learn to discern His true voice, as never before. Likewise, a clear distinction must be developed in our maturity to rightly appropriate the proper level of authority and dimension of our spiritual experiences. Clearly, the Lord desires to touch and embrace His people. Nevertheless, we should be careful not to call things Throne Room revelations and visitations that are not from that lofty place.

Our directive is to guard, through the Holy Spirit, the great treasure entrusted to us. We cannot afford to devalue our spiritual currency at this crucial stage, nor abort or even delay this marvelous opportunity.

UNPRECEDENTED OPPORTUNITIES

We are living in a day unprecedented in history. Great and divine opportunities are imminently before us as many mysteries of the Kingdom are beginning to unfold. The prophet Daniel foresaw this day and was instructed to seal the revelation of his vision for, "the time of the end." We are living in that day and the seal is being lifted from the revelation of end time promises. One of the most notable opportunities being given to His Church is the "open door" presented in Revelations.

Revelations 4:1 After this I looked, and, behold, a door *was* opened in heaven: and the first voice which I heard *was* as it were of a trumpet talking with me; which said, Come up hither, and I will shew thee things which must be hereafter.

A body of righteous believers is being given the invitation to "come up here" that He might disclose things that will be taking place in this generation. There are many within the Church who is earnestly calling upon the Lord, corporately and individually, that: He will answer you, and show you great and mighty things, which you do not know.

Jeremiah 33:3 Call unto me, and I will answer thee, and shew thee great and mighty things, which thou knowest not.

A careful examination of the language in this passage discloses that it is referring to truth hidden and wisely set apart for a specific time in the scheme of God. As we "call" He will "show." This is a divine invitation that cannot be approached carelessly, presumptuously or flippantly. It is a sacred and holy mandate that must be addressed with the greatest reverence and awe. It is essential that we are equipped with the discernment and maturity to recognize a forged imitation presented with the intent to deceive. The manna reserved for this day to unfold the Kingdom of Heaven is of priceless value. The one whose misguided desire to "be like the Most High," will attempt, with keen earnest, to keep us from it by appealing to the imagination and wounds of the people in the arena of the soul. It is our devoted pursuit to encounter God in this dimension by responding to this incredible opportunity. It was overwhelming to me, and remains so today, to think that the Creator of the universe would give me, or any man, an invitation and opportunity to encounter Him in a face to face exchange. Even so, we want truth and the fruit of genuine Third Heaven encounters, which are grounded in the Scriptures, bearing the seal and endorsement of God.

OUR WARNING

No doubt history will support that our adversary will attempt to propel this reality beyond its prescribed

Biblical parameters. The faithful stewardship of this great responsibility falls upon those who are pursuing this dimension in God. Both the Scriptures and Church history provide illuminating attributes and fruit generated when encountering the Lord in such an awesome way. This will help us to judge the authenticity of a true Third Heaven experience and separate it from the excessive and fanatical. One of the most often quoted passages in Scripture involves the righteous prophet Isaiah and his opportunity to ascend to the Third Heaven and encounter God in a "Throne Room" experience.

Isaiah 6:1 In the year that king Uzziah died I saw also the Lord sitting upon a throne, high and lifted up, and his train filled the temple.

Isaiah 6:5 Then said I, Woe *is* me! for I am undone; because I *am* a man of unclean lips, and I dwell in the midst of a people of unclean lips: for mine eyes have seen the King, the LORD of hosts.

Because of his humility, an atoning provision was offered providing the cleansing he needed to stand in this place. Much is written about this notable prophet and his standard of righteousness and commitment to the God of Israel. Both the Scriptures and history record his stand against the apostasy and infidelity of God's covenant people.

In fact, it is commonly believed that his position of purity to the truth cost him his life. It is believed and recorded, that he was torn asunder because he refused to compromise. By no means do we suggest that access is granted to this Heavenly domain by virtue of any works or merits of our own. Rather, it is by the grace of God and our willingness to yield to the consecrating work of the Holy Spirit. Likewise, such an opportunity is not approached carelessly. It requires devoted stewardship. There are many who are pursuing this worthy goal in corporate meetings. Nonetheless, our counsel is to be observant that the genuine does not get lost in the counterfeit. The judicious administration of this aspect in Him will require governmental oversight from those anointed with the Spirit of Wisdom and Revelation. The evidence and fruit of Isaiah's experience is vividly portrayed in this Biblical account. No doubt, Isaiah had been given the privilege of seeing numerous visions and revelations of the Lord in his office as prophet. He was functioning in his prophetic calling long before his visit to the Throne of Heaven. Even so, the power and unveiling of God in this experience left Isaiah, according to his own words, undone and ruined. It no doubt left an indelible mark on his life and character.

EQUIPPING WARRIORS

Our national military has now developed sophisticated state-of-the-art weaponry that is off-the-charts in its versatility and effectiveness.

That is a natural indication of a spiritual reality. What an incredible waste it would be, of both manpower and armament, if our armed forces took a rookie, fresh out of boot camp and outfitted him with these weapons and sent him to the front line. Most likely, he would be killed and the valuable weapons lost, so is it in the Lord's Kingdom.

There is a place of growth and maturity required to be entrusted with "advanced weaponry" so the warrior would not be killed or the weapons lost. With mass media and all the varied and simple means at our disposal to "approach the front-lines," it would be virtually effortless for people with developing gifts to engage the enemy in a realm beyond their maturity and scope of authority. The Lord loves us and has plans for our welfare and not our tragedy or demise. He has provided imperative equipping ministries that afford a place to develop in our gifts and callings and discover the Lord's weapons and how to us them efficiently and where our zeal is tempered with wisdom.

Ephesians 4:12 For the perfecting of the saints, for the work of the ministry, for the edifying of the body of Christ:

The term "equipping or perfecting" in this passage is "katartisismos," denoting—to make fit and implying a process leading to consummation... a fitting or preparing fully and perfecting; to be fully furnished.

This expression emphasizes a work to be taken to its completion, without leaving that place until fully furnished. In this stage of our development, we also discover His intimacy and fellowship as we cultivate exchange with Him and learn to hear His Voice then another we will not follow. Truthfully, this is a wonderful place that should not be speedily departed. It would be like Paul and Barnabas, who while praying and ministering to the Lord, were set apart by the Holy Spirit and Sent. Then it is the Lord's command and He will cover and protect His purpose. In The Spirit Presently, there are many in the Church who are oppressed with feelings of hopelessness, fear, doubt and other burdensome influences exploited by the enemy. It is the purpose and desire of the Holy Spirit to carry believers above this realm, into the Spirit, where our blessings and provisions are discovered in Christ. In this place we embrace hope to displace hopelessness and fear is overcome by faith. This truth is evident in both the Old and New Testament. On one occasion, the prophet Elisha boldly encountered the Army's of the king of Aram. On the other hand, his servant was battling issues of fear and doubt. That is, until he was carried above that realm to discover the more accurate spiritual perspective. God's governmental leader helped the lad above the soul realm of fear and doubt by saying:

2 Kings 6:16, 17 And he answered, Fear not: for they that *be* with us *are* more than they that *be* with them. And Elisha prayed, and said, LORD, I pray thee, open his eyes, that he may see. And the LORD opened the eyes of the young man; and he saw: and, behold, the mountain *was* full of horses and chariots of fire round about Elisha.

Then the prophet prayed for his servant, the impartation of the anointing allowed the servant access to the realm of faith and supernatural vision. As a result, he was changed and his perspective radically transformed. The deceptive view he previously held is the only one our adversary wants us to comprehend. When we walk by the Spirit, we will not carry out the deeds of the fallen nature. The experience produced genuine and evident change in the servant. His life was radically affected. The Example of Maria Woodworth-Etter Visions and revelations seemed to be an integral part of the ministry of Maria Woodworth-Etter. This realm of the Holy Spirit was experienced by those who were saved and others who attended the meetings to ridicule and mock her ministry. It is well documented that many saints who were bound by various forms of oppression and sickness were delivered through their supernatural encounter with the Heavenly realm during these meetings. In each meeting in which this dimension was opened, a reverential awe permeated the auditorium and forever changed each one it touched. Lifelong commitments to the Lord were made by many individuals who discovered that "open door" in her meetings. It is reported that some actually received the gift of speaking other languages and commissioned as missionaries to the nations. Woodworth-Etter reported that prophetic utterances were given to young and old alike concerning future events, many of which took place within days or weeks of the experience. Others returned with supernatural knowledge and insight that they had no way of knowing within themselves. In each case, the people were captured by the humility and contrition demonstrated by those given this great opportunity to encounter God in this spiritual arena. There was no boasting or superficial behavior, only reverence, contrition and commitments to lives of consecration. Even so, great joy also characterized her life and ministry. In one particular meeting in St. Louis, Missouri, the people of the city were particularly harsh in their treatment of this precious sister and her ministry team. The meetings were attended by some of the most hardened characters in the city. Woodworth-Etter wrote, "men stood on the seats with hats on, cigars and pipes in their mouths, coats off and sleeves rolled up...women wore dirty aprons...and bare armed...they would shoot off firecrackers and when we sang they sang even louder and when we prayed they clapped their hands and cheered. They carry pistols and clubs and were ready to kill us and tear down the tent. The end of the story is quite different. The Lord faithfully heard the prayer of His devoted saints and responded by opening the Heavens and giving the people visions of Heaven and hell. They encountered the spiritual dimension opened to them by the Holy Spirit. The results were, according to Woodworth-Etter, "the fear of God came upon the multitude. The sweat came on their faces and they stood as though in a trance; men began to take their pipes out of their mouths and their hats off. The women began to cover their bare necks and arms with aprons. They felt they stood naked and guilty before God. They began to get off the seats (from standing) and sit down but some fell and lay like dead." The evidence of a tangible touch from the "Third Heaven" was evident and easily discerned. This was true both for those who were saved and those who were not. The fruit was apparent by the responses of the people.

It is often recorded in Woodworth-Etter's writings that sinners and saints alike, would often cry out in reverential fear when the Heavenly dimension was opened to them.

ANGELIC PROVISION

This is a Chapter you need to be open to the possibilities. I believe that there are Angels directly connected to the financial realm. The Church is in need for supernatural provision and we must accept the angels that bring that release.

ANGELS RELEASE FINANCES

Not only does God have many angels on assignment, but there is an angelic realm in heaven devoted to finances. Why? It's because God oversees the wealth of this world and He has certain proven strategies in place. After all, it's His wealth, no matter whose hands it's in. His angels are on assignment to watch over your finances, to gather money, to gather investments, to bring favor, and to bring power in your life so that you can have favor and wealth. He wants to provide for you! One of His names is Jehovah Jireh, which means God our provider.

I've had a visitation from the Lord in which I've seen the angel of finance. Every time this happens (in our meetings) there is an incredible financial breakthrough something is opened up in heaven, it invades the earth, and people respond by giving generously. And afterward many testimonies come in reporting the abundant blessings that people have received in return!

There has been multiple times when we took offerings that after seeing this angel something happened in the offering. I will share three times that I saw this angel. The first and second is after taking the offering, there was one envelope that was over filled. After we took the money out of the envelope, it was more than the size of that envelope. The first time as we counted there was hundred dollar bills, twenties, tens etc. We counted it and it was near two thousand dollars in an assortment of wadded up bills. The next time the amount was near a thousand dollars in wadded bills. WOW! I wouldn't believe it if I didn't see it for myself. The third time I saw the angel there was ten one hundred dollar bills would fall around the pulpit as I preached in a meeting.

There was a woman whom had been coming to my meetings during this time of supernatural provision. She was at home and reported a hundred dollar bill in her bible. We had other reports in women's purses and I believe we have seen nothing yet.

Scripture also speaks of an angel that releases finances. I understand that God will supply all my need according to His riches in glory.

Philippians 4:19 But my God shall supply all your need according to his riches in glory by Christ Jesus.

Do you know what that means? There are riches in glory because the earth is the Lord's and everything in it.

He is the God who supplies our needs according to His riches in glory. The bible even tells us that the silver and gold is His. So when I need a financial breakthrough I don't just pray and ask God for my financial breakthrough. I go into intercession and become a partner with the angels by petitioning the Father for the angels that are assigned to getting me money: "Father, give me the angels in heaven right now that are assigned to get me money and wealth. And let those angels be released on my behalf. Let them go into the four corners of the earth and gather me money. Let them gather my partners." You know why it's important to pray like this? Because the Devil wants to cut off your cash flow. He wants to hinder and block your finances. He wants to do whatever he can to hinder you from receiving the blessing and provision that God has for you. Sometimes praying about it isn't good enough because you need to prevail in heaven where the angels and demons are actually fighting. We want to push back the demonic forces, so sometimes we need to say, "Father, let those legions of angels assigned to release financial breakthrough, come into the earth right now and loose the Devil from the money assigned to me. I call in that money in the name of Jesus." Sometimes when I pray this way,... I've got the money I need within a few days. Yes, I get financial breakthrough because God is my source. If man doesn't have it for me, God does. Yet the Devil is trying to keep it from getting to me. Even though God heard me on the first day, the Devil wants to delay it 21 days or as long as he can. But I've got to get the angels involved with my incense (heart of my worship) and say, come on God, let those angels come and help fulfill Your Word You promised me the blessing of the Lord that makes one rich and You add no sorrow with it.

The encounters with the angel of finance, is an excellent example of heaven's realities. I believe that the signs and wonders are brought by angels. I'm talking about gemstones, gold dust, and even gold fillings. It was all blessing upon blessing on earth as it is in heaven! Pondering all that happened in the meetings, I asked God, "Why was that some offerings so supernatural?" Here's what He told me: "It was because you went into heaven and by a revelation you got the offering in the spirit realm. So it showed up in the natural realm." Not only was those offerings affected by a spirit of giving, the people were affected too, to the point that they poured out financial blessings freely on each other!

ANGEL OF THE PROPHETIC

When God brings this supernatural release from His Glory, we must not try to horde the provision. There was a time when the gemstones came in abundance, when we kept them for our selves it killed the revival. One woman that received a hundred dollar bill blessed someone who was in need. We must keep our heart right. When God provides an increase become an increased blessing through giving. God will always bring more and there is enough for everyone if we just keep our heart right.

ABOUT THE AUTHOR

Bill Vincent was born 12/25/73 in Illinois. Bill had a lot of challenges as a child. Bill was the teenager parents didn't want their children to hang with. Bill was invited to a prophetic service about 1990 and after he went that was the service that changed his life. Bill was born again and ministered to for the first time. The man that prophesied to Bill that day was Dennis Goodell of International Miracle Ministries. Dennis Goodell has now gone on to be with the Lord.

Bill was a servant to Dennis Goodell for about ten years and had seen and experienced a great deal of miracles. This was the man Bill received an impartation of gifts of the Holy Spirit.

Bill was trained within the Church for many years. Bill's prophetic gift was matured and sharpened. Bill was ordained in 2001 while being a minister within the Church. Bill continued ministering in the Church and other places. In 2001 Bill established a Church in Litchfield, IL.

This ministry traveled as the Lord led. Bill operated in the prophetic with words of knowledge for healing spirit, soul and body. In 2008 Bill was frustrated and sought God for something fresh. After a couple of months God showed up with His mighty presence. August 2008 a Revival started. God's presence got stronger and stronger. After a few months God began to show up with mighty miracles, healing, signs and wonders. The revival continued for over two years. There were many miracles and signs every week. There were testimonies of Cancers healed, tumors removed, arthritis healed and many other creative miracles.

Bill has an accurate prophetic gift, a powerful revelatory preaching anointing with miracles signs and wonders following.

Bill started a ministry by the name of Revival Waves of Glory Ministries in 2010. This ministry is a ministry with a fresh vision. God has brought Bill through much adversity. This ministry has already had signs and wonders with deep prophetic ministry. Bill is a Prophet of God with a true Apostolic Anointing. Bill has authored many books, established a School of ministry called The School of the Supernatural and created a book publishing company called Revival Waves of Glory Books & Publishing.

Bill has found the glory of God in an awesome way. He has a special relationship with the father and powerful revelatory, healing and prophetic anointings.

RECOMMENDED PRODUCTS

By Bill Vincent
Overcoming Obstacles
Uncovering God's Glory
Defeating the Demonic Realm
Increasing Your Prophetic Gift
A Greater Anointing
Receiving Your Miracle
The Supernatural Ream
Waves of Revival
Revelatory Restoration
Resurrection Power
Called of God
Discovering Breakthrough
Increasing God's Glory
Love is Waiting—Don't Let Love Pass You By
Signs & Wonders
Healing Training Manual
Rapture Revelations
Expanding God's Glory

By Bishop Gregory Leachman
God's Greatest Challenge:
Man & His Ungodly Ways

By Richard Money
My Life in a Salami Factory

CONTACT THE AUTHOR

Bill Vincent
Revival Waves of Glory Ministries
PO Box 596
Litchfield, IL 62056

SD - #0023 - 070726 - C0 - 216/138/6 - PB - 9780692658154 - Gloss Lamination